Unveiling the Breath:

One woman's journey into understanding Islam and gender equality

DONNA KENNEDY-GLANS

Unveiling the Breath:
One woman's journey into understanding Islam and gender equality

Pari
Publishing

Donna Kennedy-Glans is a lawyer and businesswoman with 24 years of practical experience guiding organizations in their management of ethical dilemmas—at head office and on the ground—in more than 30 countries. She was the first female vice-president of a large Canadian-based energy company, Nexen.

At the invitation of female leaders and host governments in places such as Yemen, Egypt, Oman, India and Nepal, Kennedy-Glans founded Bridges Social Development in 2005, (www.canadabridges.com), a volunteer organization and registered charity that trains and mentors female (and male) community leaders in healthcare, law, journalism, education and politics in these countries.

Donna Kennedy-Glans lives in Calgary, Alberta, with her husband and their three sons.

And in Donna's own words:

Ground-truthing is a passion for me. I'm curious about life, and for me, the best path to understanding is through experience. That means you will find me, together with my husband and sons and friends, hiking through the peaks and valleys of the Rocky Mountains during the Canadian summers and snow-shoeing in the winter, always looking at nature up close and personal. You may also find me with a camera in hand, in the wee hours of the morning in a marketplace in Vietnam or Egypt, or anywhere, talking to people and witnessing the minute details of their daily lives.

Another favorite place for me is mucking about in the farming community where I grew up. You may find me practicing my Spanish with migrant workers from Mexico who travel to these Canadian farms to pick tobacco, enjoying a Sunday morning coffee at the farmhouse kitchen table with neighborhood farmers, or picking ripe tomatoes from the garden to can.

"Donna Kennedy-Glans brings wisdom, substance, and experience to the entrenched confusions and assumptions that stymie and harm individuals and societies, especially through the women. She guides the reader into the "breathing space" where clarity and patience unveil the "oneness," both infinitely complex and simple. There, instead of divides between women and men, secular and spiritual, East and West, and within cultures, you experience the truth of the deeper unity, richness, and potential.

We know peace depends upon educated, passionate women leading the world with their truth. Kennedy-Glans' book is not only a joy to read but it is a manual for this adventure, bringing us greater wisdom, power, leadership, and more comfort within the miracle of who we are."

Patricia Smith Melton, editor, interviewer, and photographer of *Sixty Years, Sixty Voices: Israeli and Palestinian Women*; founder and board chair of Peace X Peace ("peace by peace"); former executive director of Peace X Peace; recipient of the 2008 Rumi Forum Peace Award; recipient of a 2008 OneWorld's Person of the Year Award.

"The author draws together experiences from Yemen and her personal life into a balanced reflection on gender relations that is both encouraging and refreshing. She has winsomely combined insights from many sources but maintains an intimate focus, and persuades from experience rather than imposes views. Her most original contributions stem from her personal sharing with Yemeni Muslim women.

Scholars of Islamic culture have increasingly recognized the importance of understanding Muslims from within and in their individual variations. Although the writer is not a professional Islamicist, she has grasped this essential human truth and as a result her reporting has the ring of truth and often expresses a poignant realism. In addition to its general relevance her work will therefore need to be reckoned with in the Muslim dimension of gender studies. We look forward to more productions from this sensitive pen."

Roland E. Miller PhD, Professor Emeritus, Islamic Studies, University of Regina, Saskatchewan

"This is a timely and significant book. By exploring a different tradition we begin to realize the deeply ingrained assumptions of our own cultural behavior. Donna Kennedy-Glans offers all of us the promise of a much needed transformation."

F. David Peat PhD, author of *Gentle Action: Bringing creative change to a turbulent world*

"This book is a major step towards peace because it shows us how to understand people who appear different but are basically the same as us. It reminds me of *Uncle Tom's Cabin*. Through both gentleness and brutality, it causes ripples which change the world for the better! It's beautiful and powerful! If everyone read this book, peace would break out! Thank you, Donna, for writing such an important and inspiring book!"

Frances Wright, Founder, Famous 5 Foundation

"How can we in the West, without presumption or arrogance, help effect social change in the Islamic countries, while refining our own convictions and practices—especially in relation to gender roles? Drawing on her experiences around the world, and in the troubled but fascinating state of Yemen in particular, Donna Kennedy-Glans suggests that we have the power to reframe our own ideas about gender, while creating a new and more subtle dialogue with traditional cultures, including fundamentalist Islam. With many telling examples from her own rich personal experience, and using both traditional wisdom and some of the latest research in various fields, she advances the idea of subtle connections, respect, "breathing spaces" that would replace chauvinism and confrontation, and create dialogues from which vital new relations would emerge, both on the personal and social levels. An original book, highly-informed and intelligent, *Unveiling the Breath* should be read by anyone in search of new insights in gender relations, or in possible future paths for women in the emerging global culture."

Tom Henighan, author of *Coming of Age in Arabia: A memoir of Aden before the terror*

Pari Publishing

Via Tozzi 7, 58045 Pari (GR), Italy
www.paripublishing.com

Dedicated to my three sons

All royalties from the sale of this book will be dedicated to advancing gender harmonization through the volunteer work of Bridges Social Development (www.canadabridges.com)

Table of Contents

Muslim woman with hoopoe bird. Lynnie Wonfor

It was on you King Solomom relied
To carry secret messages between
His court and distant Sheba's lovely queen.

Reference to the hoopoe bird from "The Conference of the Birds" by
twelfth-century poet, Farid ud-Din Attar.

Nothing worth doing is completed in our lifetime; therefore, we must be saved by hope. Nothing true or beautiful or good makes complete sense in any immediate context of history; therefore, we must be saved by faith. Nothing we do, however virtuous, can be accomplished alone; therefore, we are saved by love.

Reinhold Niebuhr

Prologue

Poison in the Honey

We are seated at a seaside eatery in Dr Ahlam's hometown, Mulkulla, a city populated by roughly 200,000 people, located at the point where the expanse of Hadhramout's desert meets the Arabian Sea. Yemen is a beguiling country wedged into the heel of the Arabian Peninsula, caught in place and time between ultra-conservative Saudi Arabia and the razzle-dazzle of modernizing Dubai. For generations, the mud buildings of Mulkulla have stretched along Yemen's shoreline, whitewashed for stunning contrast against the blue sea. Hand-carved wooden skiffs scuttle along the shoreline, bearing fish and generations of fishermen and more recently, refugees from the Horn of Africa seeking refuge in a safer place.

Yemen's rugged Hadhramout region was once the heart of the great frankincense empire. In the days when the aroma of this precious oil sweetened every altar and funeral, frankincense was exported from this coast to Damascus, Jerusalem, Thebes, Nineveh and Rome at prices reaching one hundred times its cost. Now, this sandy coast is world-renowned for its honey, precious nectar assiduously gleaned from a harsh landscape.

The Hadhramout is also the ancestral home to the bin Ladens, a benevolent Yemeni family struggling, fervently, to disown terrorism.

The mood is holiday-like at the restaurant. Our table is laden with tin platters of grilled fish, irregular rounds of warm flatbread pitched directly onto the table, and clay bowls of creamy golden hummus and brilliant green tabbouli flecked with red pepper. The feast is haphazardly hurled onto our table by an overburdened waiter trying to impress me, the foreigner, with superfluous plates and cutlery. Locals adore the novelty of this restaurant, built to mimic an out-of-context tugboat. The name is, aptly, Al Safina, The Ship. In North America, we'd be at Red Lobster.

Ahlam and I are on the upper deck of the "ship," my blonde hair and western dress like billowing sails, conspicuous in a black sea of fully veiled local women. Young boys—those not yet mature enough to be called to the mosque—unabashedly unwind nests of spaghetti mounded in the middle of plastic-covered tables, their fingers, lips and palms shiny with tomato sauce. Mothers, grandmothers, aunts and adolescent girls furtively slip the slick spaghetti under face veils into invisible mouths. Babies squall. Ahlam is perspiring in the confines of her black polyester cocoon; it is a muggy, 33°C evening.

I'm sweltering in breathable cotton.

Our table abuts the back window of the restaurant. Ahlam and I are seated across from one another. Our gaze is drawn to the sea below, salty waves licking the sides of the simple, functional wooden dhows from which the fish we eat was no doubt caught this morning.

The sea is refreshing and rhythmic, a contrast to the commotion of traffic and people in the busy street in front of the restaurant. It is sunset, the hour of Maghreb or evening prayer and everyone is in a hurry—large trucks are impatiently revving their engines and honking their horns in a rhythmic staccato; beat-up 1960s-vintage cars are weaving haphazardly to avoid clusters of freshly scrubbed men and adolescent boys dressed in white rushing in the direction of the mosque. Women are clutching the hands of several toddlers, scrambling to find space in the few restaurants along the quayside. From this vantage point, the pedestrian traffic below the window looks like a human channel overflowing from the narrow uneven sidewalk onto the street, then back up onto the sidewalk to avoid vehicle traffic. The city of Mulkulla doesn't have a single traffic light, and slowing down at stop signs is optional; notwithstanding, traffic seems to flow within some invisible ancient labyrinth, five lanes going in all directions along a road that would at best accommodate two single and slow-moving lanes back in Canada.

This view of the sea is peaceful. I sigh, reflexively drawing my unruly hair from the nape of my perspiring neck. Waves of guilt roll over me and I let my hair fall in sweaty ringlets, trying not to meet Ahlam's eye.

"It must be hot for you," Ahlam observes.

All I can think is how black polyester absorbs heat.

"You look well," she says to me. "Your work training the teachers in Wadi Do'an was good? Did you have to wear a headscarf?"

"The training was good," I enthusiastically reply. "Very good, actually. But yes, we wore headscarves."

The deepening furrows between my eyes betray me. Ahlam frowns. Neither one of us really knows with certainty when the ends justify the means. After September 11th, Ahlam began to wear a face veil. I was surprised the first time I saw her with the full veil. She is a doctor and we both know covering her face hinders her ability to engage with patients.

Or engage with me.

"How are your plans unfolding for the new mother-child hospital?" I enquire.

"Our plans are a bit complicated, but they are firming up," she says.

Trained in mother and child health, Ahlam has worked for many years in Mulkulla's chronically underfunded mother-child health-care system. The only time she comfortably leaves Yemen is to travel to another Muslim country, to Khartoum to do her PhD and to other countries in the Gulf, always to further her cause: One in nine mothers still dies in childbirth in Yemen.

Like all Yemenis I know, Ahlam is a very quick eater. With the agile fingers of her right hand, and an impossibly flexible wrist, she expertly plucks morsels of the grilled fish from the bone, dips the fish into the hummus, and rolls the coated morsel into a chunk of flatbread. This delicacy is swept under her face veil and into her mouth. My mother pops into my mind. After cooking a hot meal on the farm—meat, vegetables she had grown herself, homemade pie— for hired men and the family, she would barely remember to eat herself.

"We have identified our equipment needs and we are gathering up supplies. Now we need to focus on how to find qualified doctors and nurses for the mother-child hospital. Just this week, the government included the hospital in the Reunification Day celebrations." I see the pain behind her optimistic words, dark shadows closing in on her brilliant vision for this hospital. "Things are so different for you."

I nod. Not as different as she thinks.

The last time Ahlam and I were together in a restaurant, we were in Yemen's capital, Sana'a, accompanied by Ahlam's teenaged daughter. Ahlam and I each have three sons, roughly the same ages.

I am grateful to Ahlam for sharing her only daughter.

"I was happy to see Ali again," I say. "He seems good. Is he enjoying med school?"

Weeks earlier, Ahlam's eldest son, Ali, 20, a third-year medical student at the local Hadhramout university, was awarded a coveted opportunity by the Government of Yemen—he was chosen to participate in an international forum for students hosted in New York City.

Just then, our harried waiter arrives with more water, and demands our dessert order. He catches me. I've been trying, discreetly, to extract parsley that has wedged between my teeth. With every other woman's mouth so well covered, this act feels obscene. He looks away.

"Dessert?" Ahlam asks. The invitation is only a formality; when I insist that I couldn't possibly eat another bite, she proceeds to order crème caramel.

The sweet arrives with the ubiquitous aromatic tea, served in palm-sized clay cups with cardamom pods floating on top.

When I'm finished eating, Ahlam purposely sets aside the fish carcass resting between us. She takes my hands, squeezing my fingers, painfully, and leans towards me. I cannot smell her breath under the veil, but I know that like mine, it must be powerfully perfumed with traces of the black pepper, chili pepper, cumin and nutmeg that were ground together in a curry to coat the fish.

"Ali," she says, tugging on the bottom of her face veil so that I catch a fleeting glimpse of her high cheekbones. "I didn't sleep the whole time he was away. I only relaxed when he phoned from Egypt, to let me know he was safely returned to the Middle East...I told him not to sit by anyone who looked like a fundamentalist, to stay away from anyone who had a beard. What if one of the security cameras saw him beside someone who was accused as a terrorist?"

"Ahlam, you must be so proud of Ali. Happy that he is studying medicine. You know how hard it is to find capable health-care workers here in Yemen," I observe.

Ahlam sighs and wrings her hands. "What if he had been profiled as a terrorist? What if the security cameras caught him sitting beside someone who is identified as a terrorist?" she asks, again. "Immigration officials spent six hours questioning him in New York."

When Ali picked me up at my hotel in Mulkulla earlier that evening—to join his mother at dinner—I remember being assured by his quiet manner. Ali is the same age as my eldest son, and bears himself as the quintessential oldest sibling. Deep and endearing dimples on his clean-shaven face punctuate the edges of a broad smile. He has inherited these deep dimples, and an even more deeply embedded compassion, from his mother. Ali wants to be a surgeon in Yemen. I think to myself as we drive along in the 4x4: if I were a patient, I would feel quite safe seeing Ali leaning over me with a scalpel in hand.

There is an expression in Yemen—"poison in the honey"—the slightest amount of poison can taint something that is otherwise sweet and good.

Ahlam insists on paying for dinner. Carefully, she scrutinizes the itemized bill, sharply rebuking the waiter. "The waiter assumed you would pay. He overcharged, thinking you wouldn't know any different."

This is the Ahlam that I am familiar with: the feisty woman who stands up to men who try to abuse position and will not stomach even the slightest whiff of corruption.

Revised bill in hand, Ahlam gathers her black purse and I toss my bulging green backpack over my shoulder and follow her down the stairs, the rubber heels of my Teva sandals sympathetically echoing the clicking of her heels.

On the bottom stair, Ahlam stumbles on the hem of her abaya and grabs the railing just in time to break her fall. I hold my breath, not sure whether to intervene. Ahlam pulls herself upright and hastily realigns her errant face veil. I wait by the door while she pays. Out of the corner of my eye, I watch her pull a thick wad of Yemeni rial notes from an envelope in her purse and meticulously count them out to a male cashier, invisible to me behind a wicket in the wall.

Ahlam opens the door to the street. Fresh from evening prayers at the mosque, Ali greets us with an assuring smile. Ahlam takes his proffered arm and we step out into the noisy street to retire for the evening. Like most women in Yemen, Ahlam is more comfortable praying in the privacy of her home.

Men have taken back the streets; black-clad women are trying their best to fade away into the night. I'm distracted by the blinging neon lights of the fake palm trees planted along the shoulders of the man-made canal that snakes through the city center. A hideous cement fountain regurgitating precious water is situated in the middle of a traffic circle, a place of honor, alongside a larger-than-life image of a moustached and stern President Saleh, supreme tribal ruler of this authoritarian regime cum democracy, dressed in military fatigues and beret.

"What did the speaker in the mosque talk about tonight, Ali?" I enquire.

Glancing at me sideways, Ali replies: "He talked about traditional relationships between men and women, and the need for mutual respect and harmony. There are a lot of conflicting opinions. It is difficult sometimes to know who is right."

More than any of Ahlam's children, Ali knew how hard it had been for female pioneers in Yemen, his mother, and his aunt, the first female engineer.

I look to Ahlam, expectantly, anticipating the defiance that I'd observed once when her daughter asked about gender roles. Ahlam had been blunt with her daughter: "You have to be very good at your job, and you have to stand up for your rights." Yet, Ahlam walks on in silence, following Ali, carefully watching her footing along the uneven sidewalk and steadfastly avoiding my eye.

I wave away a bee: it's circling menacingly over both our heads.

I have often wondered why a ship appears to be on the whole a more satisfactory possession than a woman. It is probably because, being so frail an object, precariously and visibly balanced between the elements, even the most obtuse of men realize the necessity of attention and tact at the helm.

Freya Stark, *The Southern Gates of Arabia: A journey in the Hadhramout*

Chapter 1

Introducing the Gender Onion

*If science and religion can meet in mysticism, then East
and West can meet, then man and woman can meet,
then poetry and prose can meet, then logic and love
can meet...and once this has happened, we will have
a more perfect man, more whole, more balanced.*

~ Osho

Mystical images of two-winged integration—*masculine and feminine*—
captivate me.

In my quest to expand the realm of possible equilibrium between
males and females—to see the mystical feminine in harmony with the
logical masculine—this image surfaces again and again in my mind. I
conjure up pictures of a world where it is possible for males and females
to be equal: a world where individuals are free to integrate the masculine
and the feminine into their souls.

Biologically, I'm female. I have birthed and nursed three sons. But
in Jungian theory, humans are psychological hybrids. The integrity of
the individual is violated when we are identified as either masculine
or feminine. *Anima* is the personification of feminine psychological
tendencies within a man; *animus* is the personification of masculine
tendencies within a woman. In Jungian theory, we cut off our human

potential by recognizing and developing only those symbolic qualities that correlate to the sex of our bodies.

Ironically, the Latin word for soul is *anima*.

Jungian theory resonates. Part of me is masculine expression—logical, powerful, rules-based, protector, independent. Part of me is feminine expression—nurturing, creating, community-focused, interdependent, flexible. My human identity is a kaleidoscope. I struggle to focus the image in the kaleidoscope's viewfinder, to integrate all the masculine-feminine floating bits within my individual character, to gather together the hodgepodge of identities wandering like Bedouins in and out of my life. To gather the fragments and find wholeness, we need to know how these values interrelate and sometimes combine: how we define issues; how we feel; how we act. Beyond biology, *how I am in the world* is influenced by the way I intuitively and intentionally integrate feminine and masculine attributes into my consciousness.

How we got to this place

The quest invites individual expedition into the heart of self-knowledge; not a heart of darkness, but of illumination. Ironically, Sufis encourage us to remove *inner* veils that block our view of the divine spark at our core. Though intimate, this journey is rarely self-directed nor is it entirely internalized. The howl of primal archetypes—how the world constructs gender expectations and hierarchies and projects sex-appropriate stereotypes onto men and women—can be deafening in the ordinary world.

In the world of nature we know that harmonization of male and female is essential: *Mother Earth* and *Mother Nature,* the *feminine* is creative nurturer; the *masculine* is protector of survival of the species. *Archangel Ariel*—often recognized as a caretaker of Earth in Judeo-Christian mysticism—is sometimes seen as male, sometimes female. Likewise, *Quan Yin*, the goddess of compassion, healing and unconditional love venerated by East Asian Buddhists is often seen as the patron of mothers. Yet *Quan Yin* can also be seen as representative of the masculine and feminine forces within the individual; assuming whichever gender is needed to release people from ignorance.

In Taoist philosophy, *Yin* and *Yang* are two seemingly opposing but complementary forces in the universe. *Yin* is the heavier element representing earth or water, and is representative feminine; *Yang* is the lighter element representing fire or wind, and is representative masculine. *Yin* and *Yang* do not exclude each other; each contains the seed of its opposite. Day cannot exist without night; exhalation cannot happen without inhalation.

Throughout history, we have attempted to divide the world into male experience and female experience; we speak of *opposite* sexes. Often, we collapse gender into sex. Gender polarities have been the underlying theme of much artistic, literary, mystical, psychological, theological, legal and scientific thinking and expression. Many look to anthropology for answers; how did we get to this place where the roles of men and women have become so polarized, and out of kilter? The feminine became associated with nature, while the masculine—often associated with culture—became increasingly more valued as humanity drove to exercise dominion over Mother Earth. Whatever the medium, the choice is obvious. We can either embrace gender diversity—celebrating the strength and velocity of a two-wingèd bird—or we can continue to attack one another and perpetuate more one-wingèd, crippled creatures that will never feel the wind rise beneath their wings.

And divided we fall

But, you may ask, *haven't we come a long way...baby?*
Yes...*and no.*

In the past century, our modernizing society legally recognized women as *persons*, offered women the vote, imposed affirmative action quotas, and even invited pinstriped-clad women like me into the elite power chambers of business and politics. Those who openly condoned discrimination on the basis of sex, we ostracized as social Neanderthals. With willpower and steely determination, we toppled the rotting trunks propping up traditions of sexism. These were proud moments. *But,* we can't languish here.

Our last moment in collective gender history took place nearly three decades ago, in 1979, when the United Nations rallied to create a worldwide threshold of behaviors. In the Convention on the Elimination of all Forms of Discrimination against Women, discrimination against women was defined as "any distinction, exclusion or restriction made on the basis of sex which has the effect or purpose of impairing or nullifying the recognition, enjoyment or exercise by women, irrespective of their marital status, on a basis of equality of men and women, of human rights and fundamental freedoms in the political, economic, social, cultural, civil or any other field."

I was 19 years old when this UN Convention was proclaimed; I recall the euphoria of this announcement and the celebration of its reaffirmation in Beijing in 1995. As a young woman coming into adolescence at the pinnacle of twentieth-century feminism in Canada, I believed that gender equality could and would be universal. The barricades had been raised; females (and males) could do anything. Over time, my spirit of invincibility wore thinner. Reality was disquieting, lonely, and isolating. As a career mom, I worked for two decades in the international extractive business. First a patriarchal family farm, then the oil business; what keeps attracting me to these male-dominated environments? But who could I blame when Western investors and the host government committed to gender equality but failed to embed these undertakings into practice; international advocates dogmatically touted UN Conventions on gender; and patriarchal local leaders continued to discriminate against females in their communities. Over time, the legal rights to equality guaranteed by the Canadian Charter of Rights and Freedoms and the UN declarations became more abstract, seemed nothing more than a mirage.

For me, patriarchy extended a straight-backed chair at a masculine table. Like *Athena,* the Greek goddess of war and wisdom born of her father, Zeus, I chose patriarchy. Or, maybe patriarchy chose me. But, counsels Osho, Indian mystic and spiritual teacher: At the highest peak I can become feminine. Or, perhaps my destination is simply restoring and maintaining that state of dynamic equilibrium that makes me feel energized; fully valued as a woman for my feminine *and* masculine attributes.

There are moments in history—*kairos* times perhaps—when not just individuals, but whole societies, are presented with these rare opportunities to recalibrate roles, rights and responsibilities for men and women. New choices surface from within the fog of complexity to diffuse previously intractable gender dilemmas; we take quantum steps toward restoring equilibrium.

Faithful Muslims—not the radical jihadists but the representatives of moderate Islam—are now squeezed in the tight grip of economic globalization and rising fundamentalism. Moderate Islam can no longer avoid this discussion. The oppression of women by the Taliban in Afghanistan sounded a warning bell; September 11 was a full-blown alarm. Muslims need to know if universal gender equality laws and global economics can be harmonized with beliefs about roles for men and women grounded in their Islamic faith and local cultures.

It's not just in the Muslim world our dreams elude us. The vision of equality between the sexes sparked in the nineteenth century, and rekindled in the last century, has not yet been fully translated in Western society. Despite logical and well-intended legal and economic groundwork, we struggle yet to create a just society where equality rights are reconciled with freedoms of conscience, religion, thought, belief, opinion and expression. We can't have access to a full continuum of choices if cultural and religious rights perpetually trump gender. Just when we think we have reached the tipping point in collective consciousness, the Sisyphusian boulder we have been rolling up the hill slips back to gouge our shoulder. Women who dare to question the sincerity of equality commitments are branded *feminists*, that all-encompassing indictment. Even worse, we expend precious energy smoothing over the real issues with a shallow veneer of political correctness—endless debates about whether or not women should be called *chairmen* or *aldermen*—choosing formalities over meaningful action.

In the Islamic world, fundamentalism has kept a firm foot on the feminine, suppressing her worth. In the West, we have tended to ignore distinctions between males and females, opening the door to female adaptation to masculinity. Equality of opportunity has been the focus of our struggle in the West, and this focus has condoned and even rewarded females' imitation of males, putting even greater strain on masculine-feminine balance. We are now well positioned to reframe the question, to speak of *equality of worth* of feminine and masculine.

Gender imbalance is not just an issue for women; a one-wingèd bird doesn't soar for men, either. There is a widespread belief that boys and men are by nature violent and aggressive; that boys don't need to be held or nurtured in the same way as girls; that it is good for boys to suffer and to hurt as this toughens them up in preparation for manhood. Dr Jagdeep Johal, wise counsellor to men in Canada, vehemently objects: "Our society is reluctant to recognize men as an oppressed group. The emphasis in our society is on men as agents of all oppression, for example, sexism and racism. But, it is society as a whole that plays the role of the oppressor."

Polarization

But why is this so hard; why is implementation of equality laws persistently derailed?

How have political agendas managed to obfuscate issues and polarize people from each other and themselves? It has become obvious to me that in order for political engines of any party (sometimes egged on by special interest groups with agendas) to secure power and influence, it is necessary to present their position as being in opposition to the recommendation of another group. It is nearly impossible to resist inclusion in these categories. To sort out the players in this rapidly evolving world stage—to put everyone into tidy, static pigeonholes— we attempted to define nations, political parties and individuals using conventional labels: *liberal, conservative, neoconservative, democratic, progressive, traditional, tribal.* But, old labels didn't work. So, we adopted new language to classify worldviews. Scholarly experts in many fields— politics, economics, spirituality, philosophy, human rights, culture, the military—corroborated the *clash of civilizations* theory in bound treatises filled with *isms.*

Terrorism, fundamentalism, nationalism became everyday expressions.

With few exceptions, this polarized positioning—which nearly always garners power—is done at the expense of the issue itself.

Global warming is a perfect example of this. Science could—and should—attend to research on whether or not global warming is happening in the normal course of study, since, of course, that's what scientists do. And the research outcomes would be observed with great interest by all of us going about in the world. But it is simply not necessary to prove or disprove this theory in order to take action. Moreover, the action needed is something nearly all people agree with: who would disagree with a strategy to continually take measures to protect the environment, conserve natural resources and protect our wildlife and wilderness for future generations, to the best of our ability in the short term, while making long-term plans for down the road? You will be hard pressed to find a responsible person who disagrees with this course of action, and ideas to advance these goals could readily be explored and acted upon if framed and presented properly. But the issue has been deliberately politicized—polarized—to the detriment of us all. And while we are distracted by endless posturing and ludicrous debate over theories that may never be proved, the issue has nearly been lost.

It has been hijacked, in fact.

Exactly the same is happening with gender equality.

If you look, you'll see clearly how we've been encouraged to see these divisions as normal; naturally occurring fissures. To cope, we've been convinced to compartmentalize the various facets of our lives—family, faith, community, workplace, global citizenship—and ignore the proverbial forest for the trees. But, in a post 9/11 world, dividing our lives into tidy pigeonholes is futile. As an individual, I see the world through the layers of values nurtured in the various communities to which I belong. As a lawyer and a citizen of Canada, I'm professionally and politically convinced that gender equality is an inalienable human right. As a member of an immense clan with Irish-Scottish-English heritage, agrarian middle-class roots and Protestant faith, I can't close my eyes to the legacy of expectations nearly hardwired into my DNA through generations of cumulative cultural and religious conditioning. The many communities to which I belong have differing opinions on the roles, rights and responsibilities of men and women in society.

For myself, I needed to break down these walls that divide. I needed to live *in the midst* of Empire.

There is hope. With access to the information highway at our fingertips, it is becoming more and more difficult for elite minorities to control how information is presented and to monopolize how issues are framed. This change opens the door to alternative choices.

With a front-row seat to a re-awakening of dialogue about the roles and rights of men and women in the poor and recently medieval Muslim country of Yemen, I've been surprisingly inspired. For me, Yemen is a litmus test on how Muslims across the globe are approaching the centuries-old quintessential question: *How can newly minted gender laws, universal human rights and globalization's incentives for equality be harmonized within my Islamic faith and my culture?*

The reality is that feminism and spirituality continue to knock heads more than any other two ideals, and not just in the Muslim world. I've been equally interested in the way in which these goals remain elusive in Western culture and indeed *all* cultures. Cultures are shaken by the imposed stricture—*the impossibility*—of picking one basic human right over another.

Moreover, both feminism and freedom of religion are doomed to failure until we successfully integrate them both into the same human reality, or at least include them within the same continuum of choices.

Gender Onion

This book will attempt to introduce ways to create the *breathing space* required to enable us to reframe aspects of the women's movement and allow a continuum of choices for women, *and men.* We can transform the colored floating bits in our kaleidoscope into a rainbow of options.

Navajo legend has it that a rainbow appears as a bridge to allow safe passage over the Grand Canyon.

What we need is safe passage.

I'm not advocating *my way, a way* or *the way* on gender; pluralism is vital to gender diversity. Working together—and looking intentionally at the sensitive issue of how to reconcile spirituality and cultural values with the women's movement—is *our way* to ensure that polarities don't continue to alienate women from women and women from men. The West's 1960s brand of feminism, including the paving of a secular roadway over the top of spiritual footpaths, isn't going to deliver gender equality in the Muslim world and probably not anywhere. If we don't muster the courage to soar, our aspirations for gender equality will continue to be weighed down by fear-mongering fundamentalists in the West and the preaching of inviolability of religious beliefs in the Muslim world.

Contrary to Western perception, vital questions about gender are being reframed, entrenched misconceptions are being exposed in the Islamic world, and meaningful dialogue is happening.

This book became my opportunity to take an honest look at my own hopes for gender diversity and to ask myself the really tough questions. Through this writing, I have redeemed my inherent feminine instincts. I have faith that this journey will do the same for others.

This brings me to the *Gender Onion*.

When we hold a whole unblemished onion in our hands, we can't see the inner layers. Yet we know that if we peel away the onion's skin, we will find the many fleshy layers nestled in nearly perfect alignment to create this whole onion. Likewise, when we look at an individual, we see a whole personal identity that gender influences at every layer. This identity is created through the alignment of many facets of our lives that interrelate, and like the layers of an onion, need to be dynamically held together in equilibrium to make up a functioning whole. We can virtually peel away these layers of our *Onion* starting from the outer and more secular layers—peeling deeper and deeper—until we reach the inner core, our private world. Layer by layer, we can probe gender dilemmas and continuums of choices available for the individual: in our globalizing world, in the workplace, in our communities, within our faith and spirituality, and at the core, within our family. We can lift the veils that obscure that view.

The structure of this book represents that onion. To understand our gender identity in its wholeness, we must understand the inherent tensions between the individual layers and identify how we can hold these layers together in a dynamic tension that does not compromise the integrity of any individual layer or the onion as whole. But before we can comprehend the uniting power of the whole, we need to understand the separate layers of our identity.

For Westerners, the outer layers of this onion—explored in the next two chapters—may feel a bit familiar. Western culture tends to have its focus, whether the issues are gender-related or otherwise, on the outer, more secularized layers of the onion. But, I have widened this aperture to allow us to see a more expanded horizon of gender dilemmas in the world and in the workplace.

In Chapters 4, 5 and 6, we will begin to peel away the more personal, inner layers of the Gender Onion. In the West, dialogue breaks down the farther into the onion you travel. *Yet it is at these inner layers where subtle patriarchy still exists in the West.* The Muslim world is more comfortable in dialogues that involve the inner layers of the onion, religion being the sticking point, of course, especially when religion runs up against secular values embedded in the outer layers of the onion.

It's a journey.

As I navigate the dusty roads that lead out of patriarchy, I catch myself humming the melody of singer Holly Cole's "Onion Girl"…I'm peeling back the layers of my own Gender Onion, just like an onion girl.

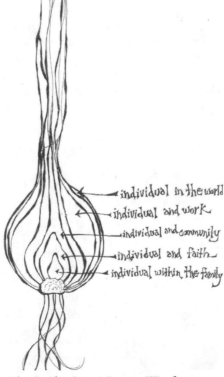

The Gender Onion. Lynnie Wonfor

The mystery of the word and answer that moves between
beings is not one of union, harmony, or even complementarity,
but of tension; for two persons never mean the same thing by
the words they use and no answer is ever fully satisfactory.…
From this tension of understanding and misunderstanding comes
the interplay of openness and closedness, expression and reserve,
that mark every genuine dialogue between person and person.

Maurice Friedman

At birth, each of us is given a particular Beginning
Place within these Four Great Directions on the
Medicine Wheel. This Starting Place gives us our
first way of perceiving things, which will then be our
easiest and more natural way throughout our lives.

Hyemeyohsts Storm, *Seven Arrows*

Chapter 2

The Individual in a Globalizing World

How I am in the world is influenced by the way I integrate feminine and masculine attributes at every layer of my being. Like an onion, my identity emerges from the inside out: nurtured at the core by relationships with family and faith; cultivated within community; honed in the workplace and molded by my wider worldview. But not surprisingly, we often judge onions (and people) not by their *insides*, but by the superficiality of their *outsides*. When someone glances at me, they see: female, healthy, middle-aged, married, mother, Caucasian, Western, Christian, professional. They try to pigeonhole me with stifling labels: token female, representative woman, working mother, Christian feminist, Western Infidel. It is the essential inner layers of my *Gender Onion* that are most obscured to others, and to reach its core, one must peel an onion *from the outside in.*

Worldview

Indigenous cultures created the Great Medicine Wheel of Life, a simple compass-like symbol bearing four great directions and a network of pathways in between. Indigenous communities intuitively understand that people perceive the world from different perspectives, and know these perspectives influence how we frame issues and how we interpret human reactions to real-life situations.

Theories abound on the rise of patriarchy and what influences our modern worldview. But in a whirlwind farewell tour at the conclusion of his term of office, Tony Blair, former British Prime Minister, offered a dead-easy approach to worldview, and one that manages to bridge the feminine-masculine dichotomy. In a globalizing and post-September 11 world, ways of seeing the world collapse into two perspectives for Blair: *open* or *closed*. People are either *open* or *closed*. Governments are either *open* or *closed*. Communities are either *open* or *closed*. An individual Democrat in the American political system can be *open* or *closed*; the same is true of a Republican in the United States, a Labour Party member in Britain, and an Aboriginal man or woman in Canada. Increasingly, our worldview is not defined by politics, religion, sex or tribe. It is deeply personal and can be simply described as *open* or *closed*. Being open or being closed isn't right or wrong. What is vital is how we hold the inherent tensions between these two seemingly contradictory worldviews.

My worldview is decidedly open; and openness leads to inclusiveness and diversity.

Value of diversity

James Surowiecki, author of *The Wisdom of Crowds*, puts his finger on the need for diversity in decision-making: *When decision-makers are too alike—in worldview and mindset—they easily fall prey to groupthink.* Gang behavior is one of most horrifying modern examples of groupthink. Collective paranoia—*us against the evil others*—can be seen in the Spanish Inquisition; the persecution and burning of heretics; the Cold War; 1950s McCarthyism in America. Foreign-policy fiascoes in the United States, including the Bay of Pigs invasion and the failure to anticipate Pearl Harbour, have been attributed to groupthink. In the marketplace, the trilogy of diversity, independence and decentralization is essential to sound investment and innovation. And, Surowiecki points out, globalization makes diversity easy: what's stopping a company or government from opening up its decision-making to men and women in different parts of the organization or different parts of the globe?

More importantly, Surowiecki points out that when a group makes a decision of any kind—as long as each member makes a truly independent decision devoid of groupthink—that group's decision is nearly always more accurate than the decision of any given individual within the group *no matter how much of an expert the individual is determined to be or how smart he or she is*. Surowiecki has confidence in the ability of the masses to govern themselves and to make inherently good decisions guarding against the dangers of elitism.

Diversity sounds like a safe bet, but does its appeal extend as far as gender diversity? It must. Again, the greater the number of unique perspectives, the more accurately a group functions. Political plans hatched in consultation with a broad spectrum of interests—not lowest common denominator concessions squeezed out in darkened backrooms, but transparent and participatory decision-making—are more apt to be implemented because people feel a sense of ownership. Rationally, we know that gender diversity is part of the richness. And emerging research is affirming: there appear to be correlations between gender diversity and country stability.

Yet media and public endorsement of female roles in political leadership feels tentative.

Lesley Hazleton, author of *Jezebel: The untold story of the Bible's harlot queen*, claims that ambitious women are given the *Jezebel treatment*, their sexuality distorted to appeal to public prejudice. It's easy to attack a female politician, Hazleton declares: "You sexualize her. Pakistan's Benazir Bhutto was dubbed, the *virgin ironpants*; Golda Meir was referred to as *the only one with balls in the Israeli Cabinet.*"

Veteran feminist Gloria Steinem reaches up, places her hands squarely on the glass ceiling, and finds it impenetrable: "Gender is probably the most restrictive force in American life, whether the question is who must be in the kitchen, or who could be in the White House." The world's focus on Hillary Clinton's run for the presidency of the United States was illustrative. The savvy Senator seemed to be having trouble deciding how to appear in public. We watched her whipsawed back and forth between two notions of womanhood: the traditionally feminine woman and the professional who can be anything, even imperial leader.

What do we expect of females in leadership; when is strength excessive?

As a businesswoman, I earned a reputation as someone who wouldn't back down from sensitive issues. When my corporate colleagues were uncomfortable talking about the reality of bribery in Vietnam, or were squeamish discussing conflicts of interest in Saskatchewan, I would find a way to get the issue on the table. In 1996, in Lagos, Nigeria, a group of Nigerian political and corporate leaders had gathered at a conference I'd helped to organize on the hot topic of how, and why, to reduce gas flaring in the Niger Delta. At the conclusion of the conference, Dr Ernest Shonekan, former President of Nigeria, clasped my shoulder and hailed me an "Iron Lady," unloading into my arms a heavy steel figure of woman welded together by a local artist. I wasn't sure if I was being lauded or damned.

Of course, Margaret Thatcher, Prime Minister of the UK from 1979 to 1990 and Leader of the Conservative Party from 1975 to 1990, the first and only woman to hold either position, is the real "Iron Lady." It was Thatcher's tough-talk on the Soviet Union that earned her this nickname: "The Russians are bent on world dominance, and they are rapidly acquiring the means to become the most powerful imperial nation the world has seen. The men in the Soviet Politburo do not have to worry about the ebb and flow of public opinion. They put guns before butter, while we put just about everything before guns." In their rebuttal, the Soviet defense ministry newspaper, *Red Star*, dubbed her the "Iron Lady." An icon was birthed.

How did Thatcher react to the warrior label? With a sense of irony. Margaret Thatcher well understood the public's mixed expectations of the fairer sex in political leadership. At times, she even seemed to orchestrate the tensions: "I stand before you tonight in my *Red Star* chiffon evening gown, my face softly made up and my fair hair gently waved… The Iron Lady of the Western World! A Cold-War warrior? Well, yes, if that is how they wish to interpret my defence of values and freedoms fundamental to our way of life."

While there's no doubt many "strong" women (and men) have had to claw their way to the top, breaking ground in a competitive world, perceptiveness is vital. When are females being demonized for their particular ambitions and tactics (when is their gender being used to discriminate), and when are females overcompensating, being forced or choosing to give up femininity in order to compete in a man's world— something problematic for both sexes?

In Canada, it's a challenge for political parties to attract females. The first time females were able to vote and run as candidates in a national election in Canada was 1921. Despite these decades of opportunity, females remain significantly underrepresented in Canada's Parliament and in provincial legislatures. Friends in the Middle East and Africa don't believe me that only 64 women were elected in Canada's 2006 federal election campaign (just less than 21 percent of all those elected), and only 68 women were elected to Canada's 308-seat House of Commons in 2008. Anne McLellan, one of Canada's most senior female political leaders, has talked to women across Canada to understand why. Women see political leadership a challenge to reconcile with family life. Women see politics as blood sport, and they are turned off by the media's appetite to denigrate female politicians; to focus on hairstyles rather than substantive performance.

Notwithstanding this obvious under-representation, deliberations about the role of the Canadian Ministry responsible for Status of Women remain heated. Some recommend an end to funding of women's organizations that do lobbying, advocacy or general research on rights issues, and encourage instead support to skills training and mentoring programs for women. Others are outraged by the assumption that activism is no longer necessary to support gender equality in Canada: *Your judgment, guided by your conservative ideology, is that systemic discrimination doesn't exist. In other words: fend for yourselves.* It strikes me as oddly synchronistic that precisely the same questions are being debated in the Muslim world.

It's not easy to measure the impact of proportionate female-male leadership in government. Most of our *knowing* about the value of gender diversity is anecdotal. It is tough to pin down exactly how the lives of citizens in a country are compromised when females are not proportionally represented in the exercise of political power. As a sex, do females have a different worldview? Do female leaders care more than their male counterparts about social issues and less about economics, or is it the public that reinforces these stereotypes with ideals of femininity and motherhood? How does a community benefit from gender diversity in politics and worldview? And do globalization and rising fundamentalism have any bearing on these issues?

Whenever I get the chance to observe a female political leader in action, I look for the patterns. In a 2008 meeting with Sylvia Ssinabulya, Member of Parliament in Uganda, Sylvia shared what motivated her to leave a career in teaching to champion the transformation of one Millennium Development Goal—the reduction of maternal mortality—into a crusade to *Save the Mothers.* "In Uganda, everyone knows someone who has died in childbirth. Rationally, we all know the statistics, yet we don't do anything to change our reality. Passing more government policies, without action, isn't working."

Collaborating with other female politicians elected under the Ugandan government's 30 percent female-gender quota, Sylvia has used this political power to drive the government policy of safe motherhood deep, infusing all aspects of society with a change in thinking about what is acceptable for Uganda's mothers. To assure commitment, Sylvia invites gynecologists and obstetricians to Uganda's Parliament to explain the clinical challenges of pregnancy and birthing, and "field trips" to local health-care clinics are organized for male and female politicians. Sylvia's strategies as a political leader allow little space for detached indifference by men or women in this community. Ugandan citizens accept Sylvia's use of political power; she isn't using power to subordinate, but rather, to improve the well-being of others. When I ask if she believes a male politician could, or would, do the same in Uganda, Sylvia shrugs.

Globalization

Globalization is a force chiselling deep grooves into the secular layers of the *Gender Onion*. The momentum can be energizing, renewing individual connectivity to the humanity grid. Or, globalization can be an incursion cutting into the male-female status quo, transforming citizens into mere human specks in a global picture overwhelmed by multinational political alliances, security coalitions, organized religions, global markets, and even the larger-than-life personas of Bill Gates, Osama bin Laden, Oprah and Bono.

Like it or not, it is official: the world is flat. Thomas Friedman, well-travelled *New York Times* foreign-affairs columnist, hinted at the strain between universalism and indigenization in *The Lexus and the Olive Tree*: "globalization—the Lexus—is the central organizing principle of the post-cold war world, even though many individuals and nations resist by holding onto what has traditionally mattered to them—the olive tree." Many still see globalization as an attempt to promote the dominance of Western worldviews—a *Disneyfication* of all corners of the world. Yet, when you think about the American reaction to banks outsourcing call centers to India, or Chinese investors bidding for Western blue-chip companies, you realize the cultural ripples don't just flow in one direction. Globalization can be provokingly complex, however one sees the world.

Globalization spawns wide, flat, far-reaching economic hubs and networks, and democratization encourages pluralistic decision-making and authority that is more horizontal than vertical. This doesn't mean that hierarchies are necessarily evil—if I'm in surgery, I'm a lot more comfortable knowing that there is someone in charge if a quick decision needs to be made. But, there is a shake-up in hierarchical world order happening.

Technologies, and especially the internet, have allowed families to gather around television and computer screens around the globe to share on-the-ground stories about extreme fundamentalists. Now ubiquitous, mobile phones are often used to document the horrors: in April 2009, a two-minute video of a burqa-clad teenage girl being flogged by the Taliban in the Swat Valley of Pakistan sped from continent to continent via cell phone. There is no place left for the bad guys to hide, no more rocks for them to crawl under. We know all about the Taliban's brutality in Afghanistan, the cruelty of ultra-conservative clerics in Iran, the eccentricities of extreme fundamentalism in North America. Our universal reaction is intuitive, primal even. We applaud those who stand up and speak truth. The whole world condemns the violators. We share a global consciousness, a deeply rooted knowing that society suffers when

50 percent of the population is subjugated. Through the television and the internet, we see, and understand, shared symbols.

Certainly, there are leaders who feel threatened by the demise of hierarchy, especially those with self-interest in *my way* or *the way:* patriarchy is utterly dependent on a sex-based chain of command. Yet, we nearly all accept the inevitability of globalization and pluralism. Some of us are eager to embrace this brave new world. And most of us are either open to this evolution or accept that there is no going back. It is like birthing a baby; once you have started into labor, you just have to keep breathing.

Reconciling universality and indigenous values

But the endorsement of homogeneous values—including universal women's rights prescribed by the United Nations—can have an imperialistic feel. Australian academic Mel Gray warns of this perspective, particularly in post-colonial communities in Africa and Asia: "[There is]…an implicit assumption that developing countries were incapable of finding their own models. Thus, diverse, indigenous forms…unique to their specific cultural contexts, were 'silenced, devalued, displaced, ignored, made invisible and disqualified'…as inferior to Western… knowledge and practice." We need to step outside our Western paradigms, Gray recommends, to view international situations through a cultural lens, and with humility.

Even with the best of intentions, this isn't easy.

In Canada, we struggle to clarify who has the authority to set gender equality standards within First Nations, Métis and Inuit communities. This is a political *hot potato* that we've been tossing around for decades in North America. Until revised in 1985, the Indian Act (a federal Canadian statute) denied Aboriginal women the right to retain or regain their status within Aboriginal communities after *marrying out,* and denied status to the children of such a marriage. Canada has a Human Rights Act that makes it illegal to discriminate on the basis of sex. Yet to accommodate Aboriginal values, this Act exempts our First Nations communities.

Many in North America try to see this issue through a cultural lens. But, a static solution, *a one-time fix,* is elusive. Phil Fontaine, National Chief of the Assembly of First Nations in Canada, passionately reframes the issues from First Nations' perspective: "The politics of blaming, naming and shaming First Nations and our organizations and painting us as wasteful, errant, criminal, stagnant, backward and irrelevant is counter-productive, reactionary and irresponsible…. We need to shift how we frame the issue… We cannot trade economic success for cultural poverty; it is not an either/or strategy."

The notion of feminism—dividing the world into masculine and feminine—can be offensive to the more holistic worldview of most Aboriginal people. Language is an obstacle. In North America, some Aboriginal languages don't even have words for male and female. Traditional values—lodged deep within the *Gender Onion*—have the propensity to reinforce patriarchal band councils and formal decision-making that marginalizes female Aboriginals. In 2007, the Indian Affairs Minister in Canada proposed to repeal the thirty-year-old section of the Canadian Human Rights Act that blocks the ability of First Nations citizens to lay discrimination claims against Chiefs and band councils. Fearing a loss of influence, some native leaders rejected this proposal as a rushed, unilateral move that could sow dissent on reserves.

The bridges between ancient symbols and present-day realities have been severed. Arthur Solomon, an Ojibway elder, laments the divides in his prayer. "Look at our brokenness…only the human family has strayed from the Sacred Way…we are the ones who are divided."

East meets West; sacred meets secular

Though the West finds much mystical and frightening about the Muslim world, there are Westerners, including myself, who see hope in a cross-boundary engagement on these questions about worldview and masculine-feminine harmonization. The West has legitimate experience with secularism to share with the East. And, I am intrigued by the Eastern notion that two parallel pathways to gender equilibrium—secular and sacred—can meet in infinity. Admittedly, there are real differences in culture that cannot be denied. Yet there is much we can learn from one another.

I've been travelling to Yemen since the early 1990s. My initial forays into Yemen were as a corporate executive engaged in the quest for oil. Since 2001, my travels to Yemen have been a little more intrepid. I'm the founder of Bridges, a Canadian volunteer-based humanitarian organization invited by the Government of Yemen to teach and mentor Yemen's male and female professionals. Bridges' expert volunteers share expertise with their counterparts in Yemen—doctors, nurses and midwives, lawyers and judges, journalists, teachers and politicians.

Yemen may seem an odd destination for someone wanting to learn more about universal gender equilibrium. But it's clear that conflicts in the Middle East (and the conflicts between the Islamic world and the

West in general) directly impact private relationships between genders. Thus Yemen became a mirror that reflected back to me more than a worldview of world conflict, but of personal conflict as well.

One of the things I've found is that patriarchy exists in subtle ways in the West that we might not want to acknowledge; conversely, patriarchy in the Muslim world isn't as extreme as our Western view of it, either. Which brings us closer together than most people realize. Changes in the Islamic world are happening, and when my Western counterparts argue that real change is not a possibility, I remind them that in the West women didn't enjoy freedom or rights of any significance until around 1920, less than ninety years ago.

Gender equality is in fact in its infancy.

Discerning intention

At a 2006 women's conference hosted in the United Arab Emirates by the Abu Dhabi campus of Zayed University, I can still feel the audience's stony silence following the delivery of a keynote speech by internationally acclaimed human rights lawyer, Cherie Booth, QC, wife of former Prime Minister Tony Blair. I recall feeling somewhat sympathetic to Cherie Booth's predicament, even making the effort to give her a hug after her talk. She was well-intentioned and authentically understands the power of a universal rights framework to deliver equality. The Qur'an talks a lot about the importance of intention; yet discernment of *good intentions* can be exceedingly dangerous. Government and grassroots participants at the conference—particularly those from the Middle East and North Africa region—were slighted; what they heard was a recommendation by a Western expert (not to mention the spouse of a British Prime Minister) to pave a secular super-highway destined for that mythical place named *Gender Equality* over ancient spiritual and cultural pathways.

Beyond the vagaries of language, the reaction to Cherie Booth's speech touches on another thorn hidden amidst the foliage of globalization's cheery bloom. Who has the legitimacy to set gender equality laws in the United Arab Emirates, or in any country?

To illustrate the intricacy of this cultural diversity maze, consider these Wikipedia facts: As of 2007, there were 193 internationally recognized countries in the world and 244 states that could be described as *sovereign*. But, there are at least 5000 nations in the world; by nations, I mean groups that share a common identity through language, descent or history, culture or religion. These several thousand nations are squeezed, sometimes uncomfortably, into 244 sovereign states. Nations can be stateless: Kurds, Assyrians, and Roma people (Gypsies). Nations can be restlessly seeking greater autonomy: Quebecois in Canada, Native Americans in the United States, and Catalonians in Spain.

When nations feel marginalized, they struggle to assert their unique customs and traditions. In the 1950s, British colonialists were, not surprisingly, disturbed by female genital cutting among tribes in Kenya, and banned the practice. This prohibition strengthened the tribes' opposition to colonial rule and support for the opposing guerrilla movement. The colonial legal mandate backfired; it had the contradictory result of making the practice even more common as it became a form of resistance to British rule.

Dialogue is critical. When Muslims hear Westerners advocating for universal human rights and equality, they can feel defensive. They may misinterpret these recommendations as a condemnation of Islam and discourage debate and discussion. Sadly, in some Muslim communities, women are treated as objects and pluralism does not include the female voice. In these oppressive patriarchal environments, secular human rights cannot be reconciled with a Muslim faith leader's narrow interpretation of the Qur'an. Yet for those willing to look at the intention of the Qur'an, interpretations are accessible that accommodate spiritual values and respect for human rights. Often it is the patriarchal cultural practices that need to be rooted out. Moderate Muslim men and women whom I've met, across the globe, are emphatic that women have equal rights in the Qur'an and must be respected. Relying on the Qur'an as support, Benazir Bhutto reinforced this point in *Reconciliation: Islam, democracy, and the West*, asserting that women's equality in Islam is not only defined in terms of political and social rights, but in religious rights as well. It is profoundly sad that Ms Bhutto's harmonizing voice was silenced with an assassin's bullet.

Unpacking terrorism

Just as the world was coming to grips with the implications of globalization, fundamentalist jihad thrust its angry fist into our faces. Invoking God as an ally in a war between good and evil remains a popular tactic among authoritarians. Empirical leaders in the West aren't alone in painting the world black and white; warlords across the globe like to do the same. One can become cynical observing how ethnic and tribal warlords, nationalists and religious zealots frame issues as an either-or debate to shoehorn people into unchanging categories out of self-interest. Humans like to be right; it gives us an imagined sense of moral superiority.

But, a reflexively judgmental approach—and demonization of people—precludes our ability to step back and value the wisdom of others.

Christian realist Reinhold Niebuhr encouraged a disavowal of pretension. In 1952, Niebuhr addressed the American people in his book *The Irony of American History*. The Second World War was over, thanks to the atomic bomb, and America had just become the most powerful nation on earth. Then, communism was the dragon to be slain and, with uncanny similarity to Al Qaeda, this inflexible enemy had the audacity to claim divine purpose. Niebuhr's advice to America in 1952 remains relevant: "For if we should perish, the ruthlessness of the foe would be only the secondary cause of the disaster. The primary cause would be that the strength of a giant nation was directed by eyes too blind to see all the hazards of the struggle; and the blindness would be induced not by some accident of nature or history but by hatred and vainglory."

In *Midnight in Sicily*, author Peter Robb describes the mafia in Sicily as *a parasitic presence that grew in the space between the State and the people*. This *space in between* can be fraught with anxiety; tension which can either be positively managed to create a continuum of choices for citizens or exploited for the benefit of a few. I'm reminded again of the nuggets of wisdom woven into the seemingly innocuous 2007 Commonwealth report, *Civil Paths to Peace*: "Group violence through systematic instigation is not only—perhaps not even primarily—a military challenge. It is fostered in our divisive world through capturing people's minds and loyalties, and through exploiting the allegiance of those who are wholly or partly persuaded."

Somehow, we need to create the breathing space to unpack terrorism. We need to discern between extremists zealously committed to the cause of militant Islam through state-sponsored terrorism, and those co-opted into violent jihad as a means to put food in the mouths of their hungry children.

Some people will never choose to look within, or to frame threats in ways that recognize the sameness of humanity. To judge the act and not the actor, the sin and not the sinner. And, perhaps there never is a *right* answer.

When the white knights from the West arrived in Iraq—guns blazing—to topple the evil empire of Saddam Hussein, hubris was ubiquitous. Today, people across the globe debate what seemed to many a gross mistake. Alan Greenspan, America's elder statesman of finance, published his memoirs in 2007. His explanation of the motive for the 2003 Iraq invasion is humbling: "I am saddened that it is politically inconvenient

to acknowledge what everyone knows: the Iraq war is largely about oil."
Many now echo Greenspan's sentiments.

But it's not that simple.

While the occupation of Iraq proved to be a very poor decision, it is
worth recalling how convincingly some Western governments portrayed
Iraq as an incubator for global terrorism. Albeit goaded by misleading
intelligence, many Americans, British and others genuinely believed that
Iraq held weapons of mass destruction, and in their fear they dismissed
critics of the occupation as naive.

Against this complicated backdrop of facts and fear, it is challenging to
unpack terrorism in Yemen, a country that has been a recruiting ground
and refuge for Islamic militants. To diffuse the risks on Yemeni soil, local
officials are co-opting jihadists; religious scholars are providing Islamic
re-education, jobs and money to extremists in exchange for pledges not to
carry out attacks in Yemen. Yet it's clear this policy falls short of emerging
world expectations.

To effect change, we must start a dialogue and demonizing either
the Muslim world or the West will not accomplish that. Benazir Bhutto
criticized Al-Qaeda for its use of the dialectic—their desperate provocation
of the notorious clash of civilizations in order to twist the values of a great
and noble religion and potentially set the hopes and dreams of a better
life for Muslims back a generation: "The damage was not limited to New
York, Washington, and Pennsylvania. Muslims, and the Muslim world,
became their victims, too."

But here is an important fact: *In the West, we can fail to see Muslim
women, particularly those in the Muslim-majority countries, as allies in the
war on terror.*

Thinking about Yemen's predicament triggers a resurgence of all the
questions I have ever asked about the West's role in fighting terrorism.
What can we do to prop these doors open: in Afghanistan, in Yemen,
even in our own backyard? In Britain, Hazel Blears, the Communities
Secretary, in 2008 announced that Muslim women in the UK—*the
silent majority*—will be sent on assertiveness training courses as a means
to help women stand up to extremists. The Communities Secretary's
open worldview recognizes Muslim women as strategic allies in the war
on terror; she sees their untapped potential to become a strengthened
voice of moderation. A Whitehall source echoes this opinion: "Muslim
women can have a unique moral authority at the heart of families as
sisters, mothers and friends and must be supported to play a greater role
in tackling extremist ideology."

Our humility may be the secret key. Helen Luke, renowned Jungian psychologist, lauds humility as the only way to release humanity from the tension between hubris (*I am the sun*) and inertia (*I am the helpless victim*) which we tend to disguise behind self-satisfied masks. To reclaim Western legitimacy, we need to lift these masks to outsiders and allow ourselves the breathing space required to validate our Western cultures and traditions. Humility can free us to breathe in that tense space between hubris and inertia.

We are capable of such humility.

Where to from here

Personal relationships with women in Muslim countries—communities as diverse as Indonesia, Malaysia, Pakistan, Yemen, the Emirates, Iran, Iraq, Kuwait, Libya, Algeria, Nigeria, Tanzania and more—allow me to see these women as allies. I'm heartened when a Muslim country decides to forge a secular road map for women's rights. I'm intrigued when a poor emerging democracy, Yemen for example, guarantees girls and boys equal access to elementary, secondary and post-secondary education; requires that each Ministry have a woman at the director-general level; appoints female ambassadors and female Ministers; promises a 15 percent quota for females in national politics; acknowledges violence against women in public education and health-care campaigns; tackles the rights of ultra-conservative fathers to marry off their daughters as *child brides* by constructively focusing on the negative health implications of twelve- and thirteen-year-old girls bearing children. Certainly, there is speculation about the Yemen Government's motivation for progressive women's rights. Is this a ruse to distract Western leaders, lenders and donors from the *Axis of Evil*, or is it a fiscal strategy to use women as the lubricant to jump-start the country's flagging economy now that Yemen's oil production is in decline and the country spirals ever deeper into failed-state status?

Whatever the government's motivation, when I cast aside Western paradigms and really try to see this picture through a cultural lens— *and with humility*—it becomes obvious that the greatest challenge to masculine-feminine equilibrium in Yemen, Saudi Arabia, Abu Dhabi or anywhere, is the ability of men and women to close the *performance gap*: the yawning chasm between government commitments to equality and individual citizens' ability and motivation to take ownership of these promises in real time. The people of Yemen will only be able to embed secular equality policies in practice—unveiling the potential of both men and women—once they clarify how gender diversity aligns with local Arab and tribal cultures and within Islam.

In Yemen, one of the thousands of voices now being heard is that of Lamya Al-Sakkaf, a political science student: "Islam was the first actor that brought feminism into the Arab world... The Qur'an states that people should be treated equally regardless of anything. Nevertheless politicized religious movements have been drifting away from the essence of things addressed in the Qur'an and stressing more unreliable sources to put women down for certain political agendas."

What I've observed on the ground is the feasibility of these gaps being closed—one tiny, remote and dusty town or village, wadi or dry riverbed at a time—through everyday actions that engage individual opinions and give locals a sense of involvement and control over their lives. Pluralism is a not a fad. Even in a military dictatorship, people have a need to be responsible—to not just give a resigning, half-hearted nod to official dogma on equality for males and females—but to enthusiastically get behind a policy and feel the social value of making it work.

Terrorism and globalization have, however, foisted new challenges onto the shoulders of the male-female security pact. Yet it is a dance: When do outsiders have the knowledge, the power or the legitimacy to intervene in the decisions of local leaders, especially those who are democratically elected? And, if the United Nations, NATO and other supra-national organizations are to provide the umbrellas under which we pool resources, these organizations need the mandate, and will, to flush out more honesty from member countries about motivations.

How does the male instinct to sacrifice himself—to defend his tribe—translate in a world where the enemy is terrorism? In an asymmetrical war, more brawn doesn't necessarily translate into more security. To protect families, countries and communities need to collaborate with others. Competitive capitalist economies can also affect our means of providing security. In the face of threats or disasters—health pandemics (SARS, West Nile virus, bird flu), natural disasters (earthquakes, tsunamis, tornadoes), or localized violence (crime, massacres)—we look to our communities as a protective medium that will keep our loved ones safe. Yet in a globalizing capitalist economy, we often sacrifice interdependence for independence. As the war in Iraq has proven, unilateral action is rarely effective; collaboration is critical.

In Afghanistan, for instance, males and females do have unique security concerns; they experience conflict differently and can tend to see the issues from different angles of anxiety. Men see security as necessary for development; women see development as necessary for security. As outsiders, the West sees violence directed at Afghan women—by terrorists and family members—and know these legitimate security threats compromise females' ability to engage in political decision-making and formal leadership. Women usually aren't even invited to participate in peace negotiations. In a 2007 *Foreign Affairs* article, Ambassador Swanee Hunt describes the response of a colonel at the Pentagon following the American 2003 attack on Iraq: "When I urged him to broaden his search for the future leaders of Iraq, which had yielded hundreds of men and only seven women, he responded, 'Ambassador Hunt, we'll address women's issues after we get the place secure'."

In 2008 I met Dr Sima Samar—a woman who should be nominated for a Nobel Peace Prize. Dr Samar was Minister of Women's Affairs in President Hamid Karzai's first cabinet before religious extremists chased her out, and is now heading Afghanistan's Independent Human Rights Commission. To ensure that two million girls in Afghanistan continue to have access to an education, this Afghan medical doctor has thumbed her nose at the Taliban. The more jarring image though is Dr Samar's description of the lives of the other four million girls in Afghanistan who are waiting in line, waiting for their turn to go through the transformational, magical door to school.

Westerners cringe when they hear Dr Samar's tales of life in Afghanistan—corrupt judges cutting deals with fathers to buy child brides, human rights commissions negotiating dowries with tribal grandfathers who threaten to murder their own as punishment for unsanctioned marriages, health-care facilities without resources to support high-risk pregnancies. Echoes of Yemen for me; how deep and fast-flowing is this undercurrent of patriarchy. Pleading for Westerners to remain engaged in Afghanistan, Dr Samar foists part of the load on our foreign shoulders: *Finish the job you started. You share the responsibility for the security of our families,* she warns. *If you don't deal with the security problems in Afghanistan now, you will ultimately face the same issues here in North America.* Her truths are a painful reminder to this Western audience that terrorism cannot be contained within the borders of countries; the protection of humanity is a human responsibility.

How did we react to terrorism in the West? After September 11, North American and European political leaders (largely male) beefed up policing and military forces. This protective reaction was instinctive; no one wants to be a sitting duck. Airport security checks now require the removal of shoes, jackets and belts; moisturizers, cough syrups and other liquids have to be separately bagged; and computers, cell phones and cameras must be checked for explosives. Despite the good intentions, I must confess, none of these security checks make me feel more secure in this world. I'm not convinced this reaction is uniquely female; I know many males who feel the same way.

Security aside, how can the West support these Islamic dreams of gender equilibrium? This is a very difficult question and, like other critically important issues in the twenty-first century—how we care for the environment and how we define the role of business in society—we need to move forward with actions even when we do not have all the research and all the answers. Hope requires responsible action. This is the same momentum that ultimately broke the back of opposition to the early suffragist movement in the West; that brought down slavery. That inner voice is telling us that things are out of whack in relationships between masculine and feminine. We see how patriarchy keeps trying to drive wedges between people; we know that organized religion and politics would like to cajole us into special interest pigeonholes. But, we're on to their tricks. The wool has been pulled away from our eyes. We must stop feeding these ways of thinking and the herd mentality that perpetrates their continuation if we want to be able to open up to a broader continuum of possibilities for both males and females, in the East and in the West. The West needs to find, and collaborate with, moderate Muslims and support their ability and will to liberate faith from patriarchy.

As a mother, I am hopeful about the chance for peace, stability and security—for my three sons—when I observe people thinking about we, and not them and us. When people recognize our global future as shared—as one indivisible fate—my sense of security is strengthened. Ultimately, global security is dependent on the degree to which my offspring, and youth across the world, share this worldview. We have come a long way since the numbing separation of September 11; a time when the world was not thinking much about "we". But we must work to truly collaborate in our efforts to resist extremist fundamentalism. Only in recognizing our sameness can we find an antidote to this fanaticism and self-righteousness.

In Bhutan, locals say the key to community happiness is allowing men to be compassionate and women to be wise. Sage wisdom. When I'm in a conversation with people—anywhere—strategizing about these tough issues, I'm more comfortable when both men and women are engaged in the dialogue and the decision-making. It's then that I'm tempted to peek under the tablecloth to see if, once again, it is turtles all the way down.

In order to keep one's feminine integrity, one must not look toward what one wants, but look only inside oneself and try to find the light. The danger comes when one touches reality, because the witch—who represents the world of power and prestige—will then come in and destroy everything.

Marie-Louise von Franz, *Animus and Anima in Fairytales*

That society can be thankful that neither the emancipated woman nor the prostitute propagates her own kind. It is decided that the ovum is passive and the sperm is adventurous. That in sperm is the concentrated power of man's perfect being.

Susan Griffin, *Woman and Nature: The roaring inside her*

Chapter 3

The Individual in the Workplace

Hunters/Gatherers

You've heard this all before, I know, but didn't it all start this way in the very beginning, in that ancient dance we all danced—the dance that led to the division of the ever-present labor force? And isn't our perception of this ancient division of labor at the heart of the gender dilemma still today? How we carved up these tasks eons ago seems to influence the nature of the conflict, or at least to inform it.

Of course, there are legitimate questions about our ability to know what prehistoric life was *really* like. In *Women's Work: The first 20,000 years,* Elizabeth Wayland Barber admits our tendency to idealize "rosy utopian visions of 'life before war' in a Neolithic age ruled by women totally connected to the pulse of Mother Earth." Stacked against our endless questions, Barber cautions: What we know remains small. We are stuck piecing together fragmentary facts. So it's important to take a critical look at anthropology and enduring preconceptions about the division of labor between human males and females.

Primates evolved with three distinguishing characteristics: first, forearms evolved (with those much touted opposable thumbs); second, eyesight took the place of the olfactory senses that most predators had come to depend upon; and third, and most significant, hominids developed enormous, complex brains. Big brains, of course, meant hominids were progressively smarter but physically vulnerable. Childhoods were longer, and more exacting childcare became critical to survival.

Another human distinction evolved.

With most other social predators—wolves and lions, for example— the females of the species hunt as actively as the males. Humans became the first group to leave this task primarily to the males. It's not possible to know all details of prehistoric women's lives, but Barber, and other anthropologists, make one point clear: "whether or not the community relies upon women as the chief providers of a given type of labor depends upon the compatibility of these pursuits with the demands of childcare... nowhere in the world is the rearing of children primarily the responsibility of men...". Barber's emphasis on *reliance*, not on *ability* (other than the ability to breastfeed) is essential. Females are quite able to hunt, and often do; males are quite able to cook and sew, and often do: "The question is whether the society can afford to *rely* on the women as a group for all of the hunting or all of the sewing. The answer to "hunting" (and smithing, and deep-sea fishing) is no. The answer to "sewing" (and cooking, and weaving) is yes."

At any rate, it does seem likely that human males began to delay gratification (not consuming game where it had fallen), and instead, began to routinely drag food home to those not suited for hunting (elders, some women and children)—something predators rarely do. In *The Alphabet versus the Goddess,* Leonard Shlain explains how this *sex for meat* dynamic created obvious tension between the sexes.

And, according to Shlain, there were other intricacies at play that truly set the sexes apart.

The disappearance of estrus (replaced by menstruation) in the female sex meant the human female could be receptive to a male 365 days of the year, and could even sustain sexuality after menopause. This gave the human female something of immense value to ante in her unrelenting barter for meat: continual sex. This evolution exponentially increased the availability of sexually-attractive females, and gave opportunity to more timid males in the hierarchy previously loathe to challenge the alpha male, provided, of course, that they could appeal to available females. But, what could have been more appealing to iron-starved females than meat?

And, Shlain suggests, mastery of the hunter/gatherer roles further conditioned the sexes: "while men refined the technology of killing, women made other life-enhancing cultural contributions.... Hunting demands 'cold-bloodedness' tinged with cruelty; nurturance requires emotional generosity combined with warmth."

Reinforcing these stereotypical hunter/gatherer roles, ecofeminists draw parallels between the treatment of women and the treatment of the environment by contrasting prehistoric matriarchal societies living in harmony with nature, and patriarchal societies exploiting natural resources and *raping the Earth*.

For generations, comforting parallels have been drawn between women and nature. Yet, I'm disturbed by the extrapolations. In *Woman and Nature*, Susan Griffin puts her finger on the dark side of this stereotype: "I was concerned that the ecological movement had often placed the burden for solving its problems, those that this civilization has with nature, on women…women were always being asked to clean up…the fact that man does not consider himself a part of nature, but indeed considers himself superior to matter, seemed to me to gain significance when placed against man's attitude that woman is both inferior to him and closer to nature."

In *The Myth of Matriarchal Prehistory: Why an invented past won't give women a future*, Cynthia Eller explores the dangers inherent in this enduring myth: "Relying on matriarchal myth in the face of the evidence that challenges its veracity leaves feminists open to charges of vacuousness and irrelevance that we cannot afford to court." Even more critically, Eller refocuses on the value of choice, for men and women, "the gendered stereotypes upon which matriarchal myth rests persistently work to flatten out differences among women; to exaggerate differences between women and men; and to hand women an identity that is symbolic, timeless, and archetypal, instead of giving them the freedom to craft identities that suit their individual temperaments, skills, preferences, and moral and political commitments."

There are lots of theories debated in our attempts to understand the division of labor between sexes. In day-to-day conversations, people often talk of *left-brained* and *right-brained* ways of seeing the world, making a gender connection. Shlain even makes a link to literacy, putting forward a thesis that when a critical mass of people within a society acquire literacy, especially alphabetic literacy, left hemispheric modes of thinking are reinforced at the expense of right hemispheric ones. Shlain proposes that a *holistic, simultaneous, synthetic* and *concrete* view of the world form the essential characteristics of a feminine outlook while *linear, sequential, reductionist* and *abstract* thinking define the masculine. The written word is linear and masculine; images are processed by the right brain, and, he contends, images (especially feminine ones) were stripped out of religion and world consciousness with the introduction of the alphabet—and subsequently the written word—into each culture. He claims that how information is presented, *how it is processed by the human brain*, influences our attitudes.

While Shlain makes some interesting and undisputed observations about how societies—and more importantly feminism—changed with the advent of the written word, these changes seem to be more a result of the word being *written* and pointed to as *law*. Customs and ideas prior to this time were passed by word of mouth, which meant information passed more slowly and with more personal variation, which might have had little to do with differences in brain function.

And, science is still unfolding. Relatively recent brain-scanning experiments done by Joseph Hellige, a psychologist at the University of Southern California, show that language is represented on both sides of the brain. Hellige's research reinforces the *complementary* nature of the brain hemispheres. It is clear that drawing sweeping conclusions about how the brain functions is still in its early days, and to draw conclusions that the *female* brain functions differently in this context has not been proven. Similar arguments swirl about whether performance differences between boys and girls are biochemical in nature or environmental.

Yet, we must be sure we take off our rose-tinted glasses as we piece together these shards of human history. It is alluring to envisage a revival of benevolent matriarchal society, redemption of the innate goodness of *the feminine*. Like others, I'm powerfully attracted to Jean Bolen's vision of women as peacekeepers in her *Urgent Message from Mother: Gather the women, save the world*: "Gather the women" is a message to her daughters from Mother Earth, Mother Goddess, Mother archetype... It is a call from the Sacred Feminine to bring the feminine principle into consciousness." Yet I'm leery too of the perils of a reductionist view of females (or males) through a recasting of prehistoric matriarchies as the *Golden Age of Queendoms*.

I don't want to reinforce the conflict between male-dominated and female-dominated cultures; to topple patriarchy to replace it with matriarchy; to reinforce male-female stereotypes. What I want is masculine-feminine harmonization.

Human evolution feels like a conundrum at times, but there is humor in this, and parallels to the oldest profession in the ancient ground rules seem obvious. But, perhaps not so obvious is this: While men still need sex from women (excluding the homosexual dynamic), what happens if women no longer need men for meat, but instead need men for sex and friendship? How could humans be anything but wary and off-balance during these times of rapidly changing roles?

Yet, changing we are.

Opening the door on a Brave New World

The placard over the company door read: EQUAL OPPORTUNITY EMPLOYER. The slogan was everywhere...in the headhunter's description of the job, in the company's stacks of internal policies, in my offer of employment. When invited into the headquarters of this Canadian subsidiary of an American global energy company, I had expected to find a savvy employer that valued diversity.

I should have read the fine print.

After a few months at the new job, I realized I'd jumped out of the fire into the frying pan—or maybe it was the other way around. Those sleek photos of female engineers in their hard hats and steel-toed boots shown in the Annual Report...well, I didn't ever lay eyes on the real women. When I looked more closely at the photos in the corporate Annual Report, I saw that the Board of Directors was, still, 100 percent male. They didn't look accessible, and I wondered why they hired me, a female negotiator for an international oil company. Except for the Human Resources manager who offered me the job, everyone with power and influence was male.

But it was a competitive marketplace, I told myself, the Iron Curtain had just lifted and everyone was enthusiastic about our brave new world; maybe the company did need to attract the most qualified people, regardless of sex, to keep ahead of the competitors. I was being sent to Vietnam, Algeria, Romania—places that had until now been off-limits to Western investors.

Being forthright has gotten me into a lot of trouble in my life, but I just can't seem to help it. I out-and-out asked the crusty old guy who ran the International department why he was interviewing me: *Why are you even thinking about hiring a female for this job?* He laughed, it was an honest belly laugh and in that moment, I trusted him. "The company needs a different style of negotiator; a female might be more trusted in the countries where we operate. In the macho places where we work, the last thing we need at the table is more testosterone."

Well, that seemed to fit. I warmed up to the pragmatism of this rough-and-tumble geologist. He had a career-minded daughter. He was a straightshooter. He didn't wear a starched shirt with a tie hanging down— phallic style—between the two pointed tabs. I could work for him. But, could I work in a division with so few women? I didn't want to be *one of the guys*. The thought of remaining an anomaly—some androgynous genderless being, the woman in a man's job—was tiresome.

On good days, I believed that this company was struggling to revitalize its ambitious commitments; on bad days, I was rooting for a corporate renaissance.

Six years after accepting this job offer, I was named this company's first female vice president (albeit with a skeleton staff and budget), proving to myself that I could not only survive, but thrive, in a man's world. *I could be a warrior.* In this time frame, I'd championed flextime working options for female employees, even piloting a program after the birth of my third son. I'd encouraged coworkers to consider females in the International group, drawing on positive experiences in other business and government sectors. Then, in 2001, after a decade with this company, I voluntarily resigned. Largely, without bitterness. During my tenure with this company, there had been a revitalization of equality values; a woman is now on the Board of Directors and women can now be found in the executive suite. My only regret: the International division stubbornly endured as a shrine to macho values.

Twenty years into my career, a debilitating illness—a virus contracted while working in Vietnam—knocked me flat on my back for eight months. With nothing to do but think, and heal, and pray, life extended me a precious gift—the opportunity to reevaluate my continuum of options. This forced pause—this breathing space—in my career trajectory was rejuvenating. Once healthy, I bounced off the couch to write a book on corporate integrity, to teach and mentor others, hungry to explore means to recalibrate masculine and feminine contribution in the global sandbox.

My appointment as the *token* female vice president had yielded an entirely unanticipated consequence. People outside the company invited my opinion on how to engage females in their communities; even the presidents of companies and countries. With these invitations in hand, an ambitious plan unfolded and the universe provided.

'Women's Work' around the globe

As a corporate lawyer then businesswoman representing the global interests of international extractive companies, I have worked in over thirty countries, most located in regions of the developing world where oil is plentiful; the same places where equality between males and females is often in short supply. Thomas Friedman talks of a flat world; where I was working, you could feel the tectonic plates shifting underfoot. For countries dependent on funding from the International Monetary Fund or the World Bank, conditionality was de rigueur. If a country needed money to keep afloat, government leaders had to educate their females, honor human rights, promote democracy and be transparent. One of these countries was Yemen, a beguiling country I have come to know well.

In 2002, the Government of Yemen recognized the need to set in motion its ambitious gender equality strategies. In the 1990s, Yemeni leaders embraced equality rights in education, welcoming more female students into post-secondary academic institutions. Females responded to the invitation in droves. By the turn of the twenty-first century, nearly half of the graduates of Yemen's professional schools were female. As a poor country with limited resources, Yemen recognized its conundrum; it didn't have the luxury of denying educated females access to jobs. Yet the workplace became the scene of a face-off between secular values endorsed in progressive equality laws and human rights, and spiritual values held within the private sphere of workers' faith and culture. The ground rules, that ancient (always tentative) agreement, were changing. And the skirmish between the secular and the sacred played out, with the government rarely blowing the umpire's whistle:

• It was acceptable for female nurses to treat female patients, but it wasn't acceptable for female nurses to work the night shift.

• It was acceptable for female journalists to write positive stories about domestic life in Yemen, but it wasn't acceptable for female journalists to be seen on television offering their opinions on controversial political issues.

• It was acceptable for female doctors to work as gynecologists and obstetricians, but it wasn't acceptable for a female doctor to be trained as a surgeon.

• It was acceptable for a female teacher to educate children in rural communities but only until she married and had her own children.

• It was acceptable for a female lawyer to practice competitively in a law firm as long as she accepted a disproportionate share of non-paying legal aid files.

In remote regions of the country where illiteracy rates were high or poverty is insidious, workers are often not even aware of their secular rights.

The Government of Yemen's personalized invitation to support their integration of secular and spiritual values on gender equality culminated in the launch of an independent Canadian-based humanitarian organization—Bridges Social Development. One of Bridges' first challenges was to work with the Yemeni to assess their strategy: *Did this government need to breathe new life into its equality commitments and practices, or did the country need to entirely rebirth feminist thinking? Indeed, was a female renaissance even possible within such faith-focused patriarchal communities?*

I was tempted to encourage the Yemeni government—or any developing-country government—to impose a hard-nosed human rights campaign, to use a legal anvil to wedge educated women into the workplace. After September 11, leaders in many countries may have been in a mood to capitulate. But, such an aggressive approach would undoubtedly have fanned the flames of conflict between ingrained ways of working and radical feminist reform. The only way forward was to create a breathing space—a bridge—that could safely carry ideas back and forth between the equally firm foundations of universal human rights and faith-based traditions.

Yemen lies immediately south of Saudi Arabia, a country where strict gender segregation is deeply embedded in culture and religiously blessed. Unaccompanied females are denied the most basic of liberties: the right to drive a car, to hail a cab, to shop in public. King Abdullah, the monarch of Saudi Arabia, has very recently undertaken tiny steps in the direction of easing the Kingdom's puritanical modesty laws. Saudi is worried about momentum building in support of a suffragist-style movement. To let some steam escape from an already boiling pot, King Abdullah recommends lifting the ban on female drivers, realizing of course that for safety reasons a woman has to remove her restrictive face veil to drive. This same Saudi leader has announced a ten billion dollar graduate research institute in Jidda—*the King Abdullah University of Science and Technology*—that will open its doors to allow men and women to study elbow to elbow. Other signals of reform: King Abdullah's unprecedented call for interfaith dialogue with Christians and Jews, and the staging of the kingdom's first-ever public performance of European classical music by a German quartet before a mixed gender audience.

It seems that the King is provocatively sticking a finger in the eye of the Kingdom's powerful tribes and religious institutions, and despite the conservative inconsistencies that will continually need addressing, these changes are truly harbingers of real change to come, here and in other areas of the Islamic world. I'm intrigued by the timing and the motivation for such bold changes. Arabs have fallen critically behind the globalizing world in intellectual achievement. For King Abdullah, the innovation required to launch a post-oil economy requires both male and female contribution. *Diversity is essential to survival;* laws of economics borrowed from science.

There are predictable gaps between progressive equality laws emerging in the Muslim world and citizens' traditional thinking. Our Western experience with secular human rights could support the mediation and negotiation needed to tease out rules of engagement between those in power and those seeking to influence new ways of thinking about women in the workplace. But a solitary path to equality—a secular path—wasn't a road map that would lead anywhere in a place like Yemen. Citizens in workplaces around the world struggle to reconcile the *push* of recently mandated equality laws and the *pull* of well-established patriarchal work environments. Building bridges to connect these two value systems wasn't a trivial endeavor.

Bridges' volunteers from Canada teaching in Yemen and elsewhere in the Middle East and Africa—nurses, midwives, doctors, journalists, lawyers, judges, teachers, leadership trainers, management gurus, and politicians—have gained surprising insight into our Western brand of gender equality. Mentoring their counterparts in the East has forced Bridges' volunteers to hold up a mirror to Western experience with workplace equality. The images that reflect back aren't always illuminating. Even in the West, our clearly demarcated secular superhighway to equality isn't without landmines. We struggle to hold the tensions between public laws and privately held cultural and spiritual values.

There are critics who have judged secular efforts to act on gender diversity commitments harshly, including Canada's Stephen Lewis, former United Nations special envoy for HIV/Aids in Africa: "whether it's levels of sexual violence, or HIV/Aids, or maternal mortality, or armed conflict, or economic empowerment, or parliamentary representation, women are in terrible trouble. And things are getting no better."

Private- and public-sector employers in the West have decades-old experience designing and embedding gender equality laws, sexual harassment policies and anti-discrimination guidelines. Despite the stacks of laws and policies, *intention* isn't always clear. Is the objective of this corporate or government workplace policy equality of opportunity, or identical treatment for males and females? we ask. Have we achieved the aim of equality if one woman is appointed to our Board of Directors, or do we need a minimum 30 percent, or even 50 percent female representation on the Board?

The government of Norway—political leaders whose tenacity on equality aspirations is inspirational—passed a law mandating public companies to ensure that at least 40 percent of their boards of directors are female. This law has teeth. The penalty for failure to comply may include dissolution of the company. Hardly surprising, not everyone is happy with this diversity quota. Norway's stock exchange and its main business lobby oppose the law on principle: Board members of public companies should be chosen solely on the basis of merit and experience. Some companies have even gone to the extreme measure of giving up their public status to circumvent this quota.

The Economist magazine reports that there aren't a lot of so-called *golden skirts* in Norway's business community; females occupy only 15 percent of senior positions in Norwegian companies. Cynics frown, worrying that females' lack of experience will keep these women quiet on boards. I disagree: In 2003, I was in Iran teaching business ethics to businessmen with foreign investors and local companies when a whistle-blower within Statoil—Norway's largest company and a significant investor in Iran's extractive sector—alerted the company's management team to possible illegal payments being paid to a consultant to secure contracts in Iran. That classroom of businessmen was extremely attentive. In a matter of days, Grace Reksten Skaugen and two other female directors called an extraordinary board meeting that resulted in the resignations of the chairman and the chief executive of Statoil. In 2002, *Time* magazine saluted a trio of female whistle-blowers as its *Persons of the Year*: FBI agent Coleen Rowley who called the Bureau on the carpet for ignoring evidence hinting at the September 11 terrorist attacks: Cynthia Cooper, a WorldCom vice president who told the company's board of directors about nearly $4 billion in accounting irregularities; and former Enron vice president Sherron Watkins, whose memos warning company chairman Ken Lay about accounting irregularities failed to stop Enron's collapse.

Where are all the women?

Despite decades of experience in the West with secular rights, we still have lots of questions and lots of inequality. Women constitute nearly half of the American workforce and hold more than 50 percent of management and professional positions, but in 2006 made up only 2 percent of "Fortune 500" CEOs. "Where are all the women?" asks Canada's former Deputy Prime Minister, Anne McLellan, at a 2008 lunch to celebrate women in executive leadership in Canada: *Forty years after the launch of the feminist movement in Canada, where are all the women in corporate Canada?*

Our education pipeline is full of females who are proving more academically capable than male students. Looking at emotional intelligence, and not just intellectual intelligence, females score high on networking and collaborative team skills. Yet, women falter in the workplace. Females are less likely to self-declare their interest in advancement; we see this as shameless self-promotion. Males are much more comfortable taking the risk. McLellan places her hope for the future in systematic leadership training for females in the world of business; not hit-and-miss training, but mandatory, measured commitments to whatever training is needed until the gap is closed.

Research into this question is happening. Catalyst, a US-based think tank with European and North American reach, has researched the gender stereotypes in business, asking probing questions to unearth why women in business are perceived to *take care* (supporting others and rewarding subordinates) while men *take charge* (delegating and problem-solving). These perceptions are not supported by research on actual leadership behavior; research indicates that gender is not a reliable predictor of how a person will lead. Catalyst's 2007 study, entitled *The Double-Bind Dilemma for Women in Leadership: Damned if you do, doomed if you don't*, explains the catch-22 situation for females in business: "As 'atypical leaders,' women are often perceived as going against the norms of leadership or those of femininity. Caught between impossible choices, those who try to conform to traditional—i.e. masculine—leadership behaviors are damned if they do, doomed if they don't."

When females act in ways consistent with gender stereotypes, they are seen as *too soft*; when females act in ways that are inconsistent with such stereotypes, they are judged as *too tough*. Female leaders never seem to be *just right*.

Again, Catalyst's research measures the wide divide between gender stereotypes and realities. The stereotypes don't represent reality; in fact, they misrepresent it. No matter how many women are promoted, no matter how many young women are prepared for the corporate world, Catalyst warns that if we don't tackle the real issue—the persistent stereotypes—the false dichotomy will remain. It's not women's leadership style that needs to change, it is perceptions.

After several generations of working, it is remarkable that cultural stereotypes about gender—that originate in the inner layers of the *Gender Onion*—hold women back. This research unequivocally affirms that women's leadership talent is routinely underestimated and underutilized in organizations. These false perceptions are even more salient in male-dominated fields, including engineering and law, where women are seen as even more *out of place* when measured against men who are perceived as natural leaders. The onus is on females to prove their leadership; males are seen as prototypical leaders. In *Sexual Paradox*, Susan Pinker pointedly asks the question: "Why do we keep asking ourselves why can't a woman be more like a man in the world of work, as if the male was the standard model and females the deviation?"

Gathering my own evidence on these questions over the years—with a special interest in the potential for females in international projects—has been unsettling. I too found the gap between perceptions and realities to be woefully long. The three most widely held myths that I observed were: first, the assumption that a Western female cannot possibly be effective in a foreign culture where the prevailing religious and/or cultural norms recognize significant differences in the roles of men and women; second, a woman couldn't hope to be effective in a culture where business and governance were dominated by men; and third, women are a greater security risk abroad. These three myths pretty much excluded Western women from work in Islamic countries and Latin America's macho cultures. And after September 11, the whole world became a security risk.

The reality is that a Western female working internationally is seen as a foreigner. With few exceptions, she is not expected to be governed by the same rules as local women. Several women I met with reported being treated neither as a male or female, but rather a third category of being: a *Western woman*. One US businesswoman working in Eastern Europe described her situation: "In (Eastern European country), the hosts saw me first as a representative of a specific company, then as an American… being female was way down their list."

Interestingly, the key criterion for success of a Western woman in an international setting was, overwhelmingly, the support of her home office and her own colleagues: *the perceived authority of a negotiator or company representative grows largely out of the way her own team treats her; if your own guys defer to you and take you seriously, and by words and body language show that you are the leader who speaks for the company, you will receive appropriate respect from the other side. If one member of your team rolls his eyes even once in a while, your authority is destroyed.*

What can be done to shake up the stereotypes and bias, to break the persistent cycle of females choosing to stay under the radar then being frustrated and disgruntled by the lack of public recognition for their leadership?

In a crowded suburban coffee shop, Sharon McIntyre, a savvy technology marketer and educator working in the United States and Canada, explains how she tackles the challenge: "I needed to accept that we all see the world through a gender lens. Males and females really do see the world differently. In a business setting, many female coworkers can seem friendly and collegial on the surface, but they can be competitive at a deeper level, vying for recognition in a patriarchal organization. Meanwhile, our male counterparts at work can seem quite macho, even antagonistic to one another in public. Ultimately though, most guys will rally to support each other as part of one team. Recognizing those differences and managing them directly can build a more successful working environment."

In *Gift from the Sea*, Anne Morrow Lindbergh spoke of this female propensity to swing between the two opposite poles of dependence and competition, of Victorianism and Feminism: *"Both extremes throw her off balance..."*. Even in the twenty-first century, females can cling to some deeply rooted need to compete for the attention of male power figures: fathers, bosses, husbands, the representative "alpha" male. McIntyre tries to anticipate this predisposition for competitiveness, at times even encouraging her female colleagues *to permit themselves* to assume leadership on issues that matter to them, asking: *"Why do you continue to work under the radar on an issue that means so much to you?"*

Lindbergh's conclusion? *"Woman must come of age by herself. This is the essence of 'coming of age'—to learn how to stand alone. She must learn not to depend on another, nor to feel she must prove her strength by competing with another."*

As a last resort, class action lawsuits launched against the old-boy networks by disgruntled women can trigger sweeping change in entire industries. *Hell has no fury like a woman scorned.* In 2007, Morgan Stanley paid more than $46 million US to settle a class action suit brought against the firm for discrimination in how women were trained, promoted and paid. In the same sector, Merrill Lynch paid more than $200 million US to settle a class action suit brought by female brokers in 1997, and now faces another discrimination suit by African-American brokers. Despite the attention-grabbing headlines, class action lawsuits and lucrative settlements aren't the norm. Employees who suffer discrimination often do not report incidents, even in organizations offering protection to whistleblowers. According to Legal Momentum, an American feminist advocacy group, *nearly half of all sexual assault victims in the work force are fired or lose their jobs in the year following the assault.* The exploited are left facing the Hobson's choice of keeping a job or trying to heal.

Most discrimination in the Western workplace is subtle and complicated, thus expensive to nail with a legal hammer. A friend, Barbara, shares the experience of her daughter-in-law, a professional in a powerful Chicago brokerage firm, and until recently, the firm's *Wonder Woman*. This female professional asked to spend dinner at home with her husband and young children. Although qualitatively and quantitatively assessed performance has been unaffected by this lifestyle decision, her boss eliminated a sizeable discretionary bonus as punishment for this *audacious* request. This dilemma isn't simple. Is this discrimination if male counterparts are also expected to sacrifice home life? To create a breathing space, we need to acknowledge the sacrifices men have made all along, either intentionally or because of social conditioning. If the endgame is a *level playing field*, should we make allowances for biological differences between men and women or will any differentiation perpetrate second class citizenship for women? How we frame the question is vitally important.

I'm trained as a lawyer, and I believe in social justice, but I wonder sometimes if it is even possible to *legislate* the behaviors needed to deliver equality. On juries, boards of directors and management committees, we can dictate the imperative for male and female participation. But, we can't control every aspect of decision-making; who leads and structures the deliberation, or who exerts the most persuasive influence on others. On juries in the United States, two-thirds of those selected as foremen—those who lead the discussion about guilt or innocence—are men, and during dialogue, male jurors talk far more than their female counterparts. In decision-making groups, we know that the status of the participants tends to shape speaking patterns, with higher status people speaking more than lower status participants.

My law school professors may wince to hear me admit this. Legal rights, alone, do not guarantee equality.

Underutilized resource?

The Economist magazine has suggested that women may be *the world's most underutilized resource*. Now we are talking in a language that everyone understands. *Ka-ching, ka-ching; the economic value of gender equality has registered.*

United Nations' reports on gender tally the financial cost of gender discrimination. The 2007 UN study on Asia reported that the Indian economy loses nineteen billion dollars annually (the equivalent to one percent of GDP) as a result of gender discrimination, and the total cost for the region is eighty billion dollars. These are eye-popping numbers. Volumes of research support the theory that women, given money and opportunity—access to microcredit being a perfect example—will most often invest in their families. Indeed, many believe that increasing women's economic empowerment—*anywhere*—may be the most direct route to socioeconomic progress.

In response to the needs of the marketplace, old paradigms do fall away. Male nurses and male primary school teachers are invited into occupations that fit the culturally feminine image of nurturing and caretaking. Managers in accounting firms can create more enticing *on ramps* for females who choose to leave the profession after having babies or being overlooked for promotions. Female engineers and female police officers are recruited to work at jobs stereotypically seen as masculine because they require physical strength and risk-taking.

The legal profession seems to be one of the most resistant to change. Progressive law firms are creating mentoring programs—for their male and female personnel—to allow the experienced and their protégés to talk about how centuries-old gender identities influence both individual lawyers' perceptions of what is possible and law firm assumptions. If you walked into a law school class in North America, you would observe a student population fairly equally split between males and females. If you walked into a law firm, you would likely be struck by the gender imbalance. Getting to the root cause of female attrition in the practice of law is daunting. It is tough to figure out why females leave the practice of law. Some point a finger at human resource practices; from the pinnacle of Canada's justice system, Madam Chief Justice Beverley McLachlin unabashedly blames high female attrition to legal firms' preservation of *an Edwardian male-dominated model*. Others blame the professional environment; the macho image of the workaholic lawyer—*the iron man*—is alive, and still working.

But, the solution to this dilemma isn't simple. Forcing law firms to be more flexible with females can easily engender resentment. To some, we look like we want to have our cake and eat it too. No one is really stopping females from becoming *iron women* in the practice of law: Working conditions in law firms can be oppressive for everyone, male and female. The survival of the fittest—*eat what you kill*—mentality is enduring. Think Scarlett O'Hara in that scene from *Gone with the Wind*: Scarlett has put everyone to hard work, attempting to revive and rebuild their Tara plantation home in the wake of her mother's death. Dressed in rags, Scarlett's two younger sisters, Suellen and Careen are forced to pick the withered cotton. When Suellen complains about her rough, field-hands, Scarlett retorts: *I'm not asking you to do anything I'm not doing myself!*

To unravel centuries-old stereotypes, law firms have to transparently consider how their organization's seemingly benign assumptions about female and male lawyers influence the firm's decisions and lawyers' careers. All lawyers in a firm—males, females, those with families and those without, the breadwinners and those in dual income relationships—need to come together to state all of their assumptions explicitly. And, younger generations' priorities need to be woven into that exchange of ideas—*Generation X* associates (born between 1966 and 1979) and the newest graduates, the *Millenials* (born between 1980 and 1995)— have expectations for work-life balance that can be jarring for veteran employees (born between 1922-1945) and especially, the *Baby Boomer* generation (born between 1946-1965). To re-establish trust, the bones of contention have to be picked clean.

Double-edged sword

Economics—and its tendency to commoditize—whets both sides of the double-edged sword. In economies where jobs are in short supply, females' job expectations can be seen as a threat to traditional family breadwinners. In a World Values Survey conducted in 2006, males *in all regions of the world* agreed or strongly agreed that when jobs are scarce, men should have more right to a job than a woman.

Backlash is predictable, and the resulting discrimination can be painful. Lots of women don't *have a man* to provide for them. In the coming decade, an ever-expanding youth bulge in Middle Eastern demographics will strain gender equality aspirations in the workplace. Sixty percent of the Middle Eastern population is under the age of twenty-four and unemployment is the most pressing priority for 68 percent of Arab youth. Yemen's demographics may be the most daunting in the region: Nearly 50 percent of the country's citizens are under fifteen years of age and the country's population is expected to double in the next twenty years.

Economics can be cold-hearted and calculating, ruthless even. Pornography and the garment industry can turn anybody—male or female—into a commodity. The sex industry—prostitution, strip joints, pornographic movies and magazines, websites, phone sex and other profit-making businesses—manipulates and capitalizes on both men and women. To lure customers, restaurant owners may encourage female waitresses to wear makeup and dress provocatively. One restaurant chain—*Hooters*—trades on the sex appeal of its *Hooters Girls*. Bust enhancements have even been offered to high-potential female employees. Understanding that people may consider *Hooters* a slang term for women's breasts, the restaurant's management counters negative stereotypes by arguing the double standard; their female employees have the same right as supermodels to use their natural sex appeal to earn a living. Just below the surface, there is another double standard lurking: why are sexually promiscuous females stereotypically shunned as *fallen women* while equally promiscuous males are socially condoned?

Economics can dehumanize, and can cruelly divide. When work in the home is not fiscally valued, those primarily responsible for housework and child rearing can be perceived to contribute less, not just to the economy, but also to society at large. Acrimonious battles, *Mommy Wars*, between stay-at-home mothers and mothers who work outside the home—*the soccer mom* vs. *the career mom*—can be bitterly polarizing.

When my husband and I employed a Filipina to help care for our sons, I was confused. In a globalizing world, did it really make sense for our nanny to leave her extended family behind and migrate to Canada as caregiver and housekeeper for me, another working mother? *Universal sisterhood* felt callous. Was I as guilty as middle-class Victorians in endorsing feminism from the lofty perspective of a white, Western middle-class heterosexual female?

Economics is the driver that has accelerated gender equality in Africa, the Middle East and Asia. Ultimately though, an employer's gender equality vision—in the East or in the West—cannot be singularly dependent on economics, or even a combination of laws and economics. Resiliency—for this two-wingèd bird—requires integration of the secular and the sacred values in ways that enable a continuum of choices for male and female workers.

Pinker bravely reopens the *biology is destiny debate* in *Sexual Paradox*. We have discounted this theory for the last forty years, afraid to reopen this can of worms. Yet, women with choices do not follow the path of men. Even when the barriers are removed, women don't act like men at work. Women want flexibility, job satisfaction and fun, not just market value and status. Given options, women are defecting—in droves—from the traditional male workplace. Three-quarters of the workers in the not-for-profit world are female. Despite all our efforts to lure females into science and engineering, the results have been dreary. According to Pinker's research, women with choices select more people-focused jobs.

In our modern age of birth control, live-in nannies and breast pumps, the West's secular equality crusade can lose sight of the value of compatibility between work and child rearing, for mothers and fathers. Continuing to see fathers primarily as providers, who sacrifice for the family rather than being intimately involved in the children's lives, denies men equality of lifestyle opportunities. Rewarding female workers who *act like men* compounds incompatibilities between work and child rearing. Part-time, flextime and child care leaves aren't easy for employers or coworkers to juggle. Surely though, in a world where outsourcing to India is feasible, incentives for flexibility in the workplace can be created.

Somehow, we have to reconcile human biology and equality rights in the workplace. And, fathers cannot be excluded from this reconciliation.

Affixing an emblem to the front door of your corporate headquarters—EQUAL OPPORTUNITY EMPLOYER—may be a constructive starting point for employers, but it is only that, a beginning. Non-discrimination policies can be positively influenced by top-down direction, kicked off by elites, champions in the corporate or political world. But, the real change requires hard work at the grassroots. *Anything less is indoctrination.* Workers need companies to be honest about why a gender equality policy is being endorsed. Employees need to feel safe to ask questions, to close expectation gaps between a company's intentions and commitments. As well, to the extent that an employer can recognize and close *performance gaps*, deficiencies in a company's ability or willingness to embed equality commitments in actions—*to walk the talk*—that employer will earn credibility and trust. Employees will read the sign over the door—EQUAL OPPORTUNITY EMPLOYER—and will feel, even believe, its aim. It will be a good sign.

A hero ventures forth from the world of common day
into a region of supernatural wonder: fabulous forces
are there encountered and a decisive victory is won: the
hero comes back from this mysterious adventure with
the power to bestow boons on his fellow man.

Joseph Campbell, *The Hero with a Thousand Faces*

Language is not a passive carrier of information
but an activity in its own right. Language exerts an
influence on how we think, act and perceive. In turn social
changes are reflected in transformations of language...
it becomes the task of each of us to take responsibility for
language and help to retain its power and purity.

F. David Peat, *Pathways of Chance*

Women are told from their infancy, and taught
by the example of their mothers, that a little knowledge
of human weakness, justly termed cunning, softness of
temper, outward obedience, and a scrupulous attention
to a puerile kind of propriety, will obtain for them the
protection of man; and should they be beautiful, everything
else is needless, for, at least, twenty years of their lives.

Mary Wollstonecraft, *A Vindication of the Rights of Women*

Chapter 4

The Individual within the Community

In the East

Baby Ali is ten months old and weighs less than four kilograms. An IV drip is stabbed into the vein of his inner right wrist; a grimy cloth bandage loops around it and over his thumb and palm to bind the IV in place. He is lying, limp, on his back, frail hands collapsed over his head in weary submission. Ali's tropical-hued apparel is at odds with both his size and gender—baggy fuchsia pants, a sky-blue T-shirt and a rosy pointed cap embroidered and loosely tied with a bow under his chin. Every time he sucks in air, his chest thrusts forward and his belly button disappears into the small of his back. With every exhale, his chest crumples and a distended stomach—the telltale sign of malnutrition—grows harder.

I'm in a ward of the Seiyun General Hospital in Yemen with a Bridges' pediatric emergency training team. This health-care center responds to the needs of the sick and the dying, and the newborn and the birthing, in the remote villages and camel crossings of the Hadhramout desert. When they are really sick, even the Bedouins come to this health-care center. I've been in hundreds of wards like this.

Ali never smiles and neither can I.

Ali's mother is young, and obviously poor. Even the blackness of her abaya is dulled with washing. Her dark eyes pierce me from behind the eye slits cut into her weathered face veil. As a mother, she knows her son is desperately sick. With that sixth sense universal to mothers, she must know that he is close to death. If she can get my attention, or the attention of a Western doctor or nurse, maybe this son will be saved.

Baby Ali has my full attention. Standing by this bedside, I ask the hospital's director, Dr Ibrahim Al-Kaff—a gentle and compassionate doctor from the neighboring town of Tarim—some generic question about the prevalence of malnutrition in this community.

What I desperately want is for Dr Al-Kaff to look at this baby.

Dr Al-Kaff picks up Baby Ali and I am grateful. Tenderly, he holds the baby in the crook of his arm, smiling into the wizened face, and ever so softly, the doctor caresses his stomach and chest with tiny circles. Standing beside the pair, I can see that in spite of his physical weariness, the doctor is emotionally moved by the plight of this child and his mother. Part of him is angry too; with better education, this suffering could be prevented. If literate, this young mother could have read the instructions on the tin of infant formula and wouldn't have diluted it too thinly.

If Baby Ali does not survive, this mother will return home with a broken heart and will likely be pregnant again, soon. Without education and awareness, this story will repeat itself, generation after generation.

As a younger man, Dr Al-Kaff had compared the impacts of breastfeeding versus bottle-feeding within the Muslim communities of interior Hadhramout and his research unequivocally documents the benefits of mother's milk. I've read the report—it is compelling, even drawing upon Qur'anic petitions to breastfeed. Two decades ago, Islam's faith leaders—imams—had spontaneously launched an unofficial campaign to use the mosques in Seiyun and Tarim as a place to preach to fathers about the benefits of breastfeeding. A mother who is breastfeeding is also unlikely to become pregnant. Islam's endorsement of nutrition and birth spacing: Surely, this is one of the more perfect examples of the scientific and the sacred aligning.

Tarim—Dr Al-Kaff's hometown—is said to have 360 mosques, and prides itself as the stronghold of faith in Yemen. The Al-Kaffs are the founding family of Tarim, long recognized as broad-minded and progressive. At one time, Tarim enjoyed the highest rates of infant survival in the country. Now infant, child and maternal mortality rates in Interior Hadhramout, and across Yemen, run neck-and-neck with statistics from the poorest countries of sub-Saharan Africa; officially, 75 of every 1000 infants die and the acknowledged child mortality rate is even worse at 102 per 1000 live births. According to Yemen's own Ministry of Public Health and Population, the prevalence of underweight children (under five years of age) is 46 percent.

Intervention does happen and it takes many forms—nurses, doctors and midwives at the Seiyun General Hospital will take the initiative to educate this mother on the benefits of breastfeeding, nutrition and birth spacing; the headmaster of the local school will encourage her husband to send their daughters to school, even offering up economic incentives to break traditional resistance; and local imams will reinforce these values in the mosque. What gives me genuine hope every time I am sandals-on-the-ground in Yemen is the ability to see with my own eyes that these interventions are happening. There isn't a lot of hoopla, and the slogan is never *gender equality*; this isn't politically correct feminist gobbledygook, this is hard-core transformation operating within a community and making real difference in people's lives.

In Yemen, anyone who can read a newspaper or listens to the radio is aware of Yemen's commitment to the Millennium Development Goals—sometimes these commitments are the theme of conferences for bigwigs hosted by the World Health Organization. Yet, gaps between the political commitments and on-the-ground realities continue to alarm. Walking through rural villages across Yemen, it is heartbreaking to witness the thousands of girls who are entirely deprived of education. You often see them as ghost-like apparitions in the distance, herding sheep or goats along an invisible footpath in the misty hills, or trudging along the dust-choked roadside, large plastic tubs perched on their heads, collecting wood or water for their family's daily needs. These girls become a fog, then a vapor, and finally a whisper of their potential. Access to that underground river capable of regenerating their souls has been dammed. It's hard to even discern their footprints in the sand.

For as long as I've travelled to Yemen, the country has genuinely been trying to improve access to education and literacy. The love of learning is genuine, and talking about learning is always a conversation about what one is, not what one has. Faith leaders are onside: According to Prophet Mohammed, *acquiring knowledge is compulsory for every man and woman*. Women can be scholars and the most well-known role model is Aisha, the wife of Prophet Mohammed. Notwithstanding, the combination of poverty and ultra-conservative traditions can conspire in the most confounding ways. Souad, a student from near Taiz, shrugs her shoulders as she explains why few girls attend her school: Poverty means that there is no toilet for boys or girls at the school; cultural norms for modesty dictate that it is okay for boys to pee behind the bushes but it is not okay for girls to do the same. *All that stands in the way of girls' education in this village is an outhouse.*

Fifteen years ago, I visited Pakistan for the first time; to this day, I'm haunted by whispered conversations with local women, professionals encouraged by their families to pursue post-secondary education but closed in by the walls of purdah the minute they had their first child. The pain of one woman—like me at that time, a keen female lawyer with young children—is haunting. I no longer recall her name but I'll never forget her voice: *I wish I'd never been educated,* she said. *It makes my confinement so utterly painful.* It was Margaret Mead who warned that education has made women restless and questing, even in the face of childbearing, and can lead a woman to disaster or great opportunity.

Performance gaps in health care can be even more vexing. According to the International Labor Organization (ILO), there has been only a nominal increase in Yemen's budgets for health since the Millennium Development Goals were announced. Moreover, actual expenditures have been significantly lower than approved budgets; only 16 percent of the budget was spent on health care in 2002 and 33 percent in 2003. The ILO estimates government contribution to the national health budget at only 25 percent of actual costs; the remaining 75 percent is paid out of pocket by users of health services.

Regional suasion can sometimes be quite influential in mobilizing change within individual communities. Leaders in a region can come together to tailor their commitments to gender in ways that reflect their shared geography, culture or faith. In the *New Partnership for Africa's Development*, African political leaders collectively acknowledged the unique impact of HIV/Aids on women and girls in Africa; leaders feel accountable to one another for these undertakings. The *Arab Human Development Report*, thankfully now written by Arabs, makes the link between gender equality and economics: *continued resistance to women's economic and political emancipation unequivocally hinders many Arab countries' future progress.* One of the most effective regional campaigns I've ever participated in was hosted in 2005 by then Yemeni Minister of Human Rights, Amat Al-Aleem Alsowa. Word of mouth testimony from trusted leaders in the Middle Eastern and North African region, including compelling stories about the social benefits of female judges and politicians, pulled along regional laggards reluctant to invite Muslim women into judicial or political decision-making.

Cultural violence against females

In *The Geography of Hope,* Chris Turner, a fellow Calgarian, describes the decentralized endorsement of a new idea as *rational exuberance.* What does *rational exuberance* look like? I've seen it, and it is truly inspirational: Conservative parents in a traditional Muslim community in Yemen or Tanzania acknowledging the benefits of sending their daughters to gender-segregated classrooms; well-known and trusted community leaders in villages in Congo or Nigeria—doctors at local health-care clinics, local faith leaders, small-business owners—intervening to re-characterize and deter acts of violence against local females; budgets within individual hospitals and health-care clinics in Vietnam and Cambodia being transparently allocated, and spent, in ways that reflect the needs of local families; HIV/Aids hospices for women and babies being quietly condoned by local imams in Egypt who only recently believed that the Aids scourge was punishment for immoral behavior and still believe that homosexuality warrants a death sentence.

Yet some traditions can be exasperatingly resistant to change. Female genital cutting remains a commonly practiced tradition in Somalia, Egypt, Sudan, Ethiopia and Mali. In some of these countries, the practice is nearly universal with more than 95 percent of all women having undergone the procedure. Amnesty International estimates that over 130 million women worldwide have been affected by some form of female genital cutting with over two million procedures performed every year. Hardly a marginalized practice. Migration has also introduced this tradition to Western societies where it is increasingly a criminal offence. In 2006, Khalid Adem, an Ethiopian immigrant, was the first person convicted for female genital cutting in the United States when he personally excised his two-year-old daughter's clitoris with a pair of scissors.

The practice of female genital cutting predates both Islam and Christianity. The cultural practice seems to reflect a desire to control female sexuality, and is widely accepted as having originated in Egypt and the Nile valley at the time of the Pharaohs. I'm reminded of Sigmund Freud's harsh observation in *The Dissection of the Psychical Personality*: "The only bodily organ which is really regarded as inferior is the atrophied penis, a girl's clitoris." The tradition marks a *rite of passage* from childhood to adulthood, and in certain communities, can enhance a young woman's eligibility to marry. If only a few families within a community *deprive* their daughters of this operation, these females can be disadvantaged in finding husbands.

Hard-core activists characterize the ritual as violent disfigurement, and compare genital cutting to rape or child abuse. This condemnation echoes twentieth-century colonial and missionary campaigns against the practice, and perpetuates a *victim* culture. The instinctive community response to this advocacy is defensiveness: *We don't care what outsiders think, these are our traditions.*

Other change agents choose to work from *within* traditional communities to end the practice. The well-documented success of the Tostan Project in Senegal demonstrates how citizens in local communities can voluntarily collaborate to abandon this practice. Using education, rather than cultural imperialism, men and women in Senegal have opened up the space to sensitively question their own traditions. It isn't easy to create the space to understand how the females, themselves, feel about the practice. Conversations are encouraged through dramatic recounting of the suffering—even death—that the practice of genital cutting had brought to individuals living in a village. As momentum for change reaches a *tipping point*, an entire village participates in a public ceremony to collectively reject the practice for their daughters and prospective daughters-in-law. Community collaboration to abandon the practice is vital. This indigenous approach to change invites a role for local faith leaders, to provide assurance that the practice of female genital circumcision is a custom not a religious mandate.

Spreading this positive infection—village by village—can seem painstakingly slow. After shocking footage of one girl's suffering was aired on television in 1996, doctors in Egypt were forbidden from performing female genital cutting *except under unusual circumstances.* The result: The tradition survived, but with greater focus on safety. Following this government decree, two-thirds of female circumcisions in Egypt were performed by doctors using loopholes in the legal prohibition. In June 2007, revived public outcry spurred the Egyptian government to renew its ban on female genital cutting, this time unconditionally, following the well-publicized death of eleven-year-old Bedur Shaker during a genital circumcision. Bedur's parents did not hire a traditional midwife or a local barber to *purify* their daughter; they delivered their daughter to a village medical clinic to perform the nine-dollar operation. Before the clitoris could be removed, the young girl died from the anaesthetic. As an echo to the government edict, Egypt's grand mufti—the most senior in-country official issuing Islamic legal opinions—unequivocally declared on public television: *female cutting is forbidden.*

Conservative clerics have defensively interpreted this edict as hostility to Islam. In Egypt, it seems that the forceful weight of government and faith leaders doesn't negate the need for village-by-village endorsement of this new idea. In *The Tipping Point*, Malcolm Gladwell even identifies the types of grassroots opinion leaders—whom he calls *Connectors, Mavens, and Salesmen*—uniquely qualified to influence on-the-ground practices through trusted word of mouth.

In India, female infanticide is rationalized by desperately impoverished parents on the basis that *it is better to kill her now, as a baby, than to let her suffer an unbearable life as a dowry-less bride.* Second daughters are known as *the girl born for the burial pit.* Diagnostic teams with ultrasound scanners prey on poor Indian parents: *spend 600 rupees now and save 50,000 rupees later!* Thousands of young brides in India are murdered or driven to suicide by continual harassment, even torture, by husbands and in-laws seeking to extort an enriched dowry—give me more money, a motorcycle, a color television instead of a black and white one. Dowry deaths are often staged as cooking accidents with hundreds of brides set ablaze with kerosene in *bride burnings.* Governments in India have tried—with limited success—to create *breathing spaces* both at the time of a daughter's birth and at her marriage.

Recognizing that couples use crude practices of female infanticide as a family planning option, advocates have championed education campaigns aimed at raising awareness of family planning and mother and child health risks, and to discourage early marriage, unsafe abortions and female infanticide. Scientific advancement—more reliable means of detecting the sex of a fetus and safer abortions—actually made the problem of female infanticide worse; evidence, again, of the moral blindness of unintended consequences. To tackle the dilemma from another angle, the Indian Government enacted the Dowry Prohibition Act in 1961 and more stringent laws in 1983, making it illegal to demand dowry. Yet, the laws did little to deter dowry traditions or female infanticide. In 2006, the Indian Government dug deeper, commissioning domestic violence protection officers to support harassed brides. Getting even closer to the root causes, the Indian Government recently modified property inheritance laws to permit daughters to claim equal rights to their parental property, making females less vulnerable. Faith communities in India are also urging families to moderate wedding extravagance, including dowry expectations. *Breathing spaces* are opening up in India.

In Iran, teenage rape victims are sentenced to death by hanging for *acts incompatible with chastity.* Appeals to the religious judges—to punish those who force women into adultery and not the victims—are ignored. Teenaged girls, even those impregnated by brothers and fathers and uncles, are hanged. In Saudi Arabia, King Abdullah has recently attempted to temper this brand of religious fundamentalism—overturning the draconian flogging sentence imposed by Saudi's religion-based judiciary for a victim of a gang rape. A young Saudi woman—known only as *Qatif Girl* after the area where the crime occurred—was sentenced to 200 lashes by the Saudi Ministry of Justice for being alone in a car with a man who was not her relative after being gang-raped by seven men. Justice declared the girl to be adulterous, responsible for provoking the attack with her indecent dress. It is uncommon for a Saudi ruler to challenge hard-line clerics of Wahhabi Islam; whatever the motive, it is a *breathing space*.

And in the West

Much like our Western experience in the workplace, we are increasingly aware of how medical research and health care casts males as the *representative* human body. The female body, and women's health, is very different. A minor study published in a 2008 Canadian Medical Association journal found that women complaining of knee pain are less likely than men to be recommended for total knee replacement surgery. The results demonstrate that physicians visited were twice as likely to recommend total knee replacement surgery to the male patient as opposed to the female patient. We struggle to understand these results: Do physicians take women's symptoms less seriously and attribute their pain to emotional rather than physical causes; is there an unconscious bias based on gender; or despite identical symptoms and situations, do physicians respond differently to females presenting their symptoms in a narrative style and males tending to present brief facts?

In the West, reproductive rights are at the center of much public debate. Scientific advancement poses dilemmas of the nature predicted by people like Susan Griffin in her 1978 book, *Woman and Nature:*

> ...within a mere ten to fifteen years a woman will be able to buy a tiny frozen embryo, take it to the doctor, have it implanted in her uterus, carry it for nine months, and then give birth to it as though it had been conceived in her own body. The embryo would, in effect, be sold with a guarantee that the resultant baby would be free of genetic defect. The purchaser would also be told in advance the color of the baby's eyes and hair, its sex, its probable size at maturity, and its probable IQ.

And, a woman's right to abortion remains controversial. Stephanie Garrett—a colleague in charge of the Women's Resource Center at my hometown university and a Catholic struggling to integrate official Church doctrine with her feminist identity—visited Chile in 2004 to more fully understand how Catholic feminists in that country navigate the right to abortion. What Stephanie found was a classic dilemma: In spite of strict legal prohibitions and Catholicism's rigid stance against abortion, illegal abortion remains a leading cause of maternal death in Chile. To compound the problem, Stephanie also found that women without financial resources are forced to choose less safe abortion options and predictable complications force these women to then seek medical attention in public hospitals. Health-care providers are mandated to report these women to the criminal justice system, triggering even more dilemmas. The dominoes just keep falling.

In secular countries in North America and Europe where abortion is permitted by law, Catholics face a fork in the gender road. They can heed faith-based leadership, ignoring permissive secular abortion laws, or they can choose to accept legally based rights to abortion and tackle the moral issue in the confessional. Up close, reality isn't this clinical. In hospitals in the West, I've seen couples caught in this searing crossfire of science and religion. What fork in the road do you take? The medical advice of your family doctor—*an abortion will save the mother's life*—or the solemn admonition of your family priest—*abortion is a mortal sin.*

Andrew Coyne, national editor of *Maclean's* magazine, begs us to democratically debate abortion policy even knowing the debate would be scary...*filled with emotions, invective, and gross oversimplifications.* "Anything's better than the head-shaking, fingers-in-the-ears, nana-nana barracking that goes on now."

In a Catholic country like Chile, where abortion is prohibited by law in every circumstance, it is even more daunting for women to advocate their human right to make personal choices about their own bodies in the face of opposing forces anchored in both law and faith. To create this breathing space for constructive dialogue, Stephanie saw how Catholics in Chile asked questions about authority: who has the authority to speak about abortion; to control women's bodies; to interpret Catholic doctrine? Exploring authority encourages not only the opinions of male and female theologians, but as well, the voices of Catholics within the community at large. In this way, a range of perspectives on choices for a Catholic woman could be made available.

Stephanie was also moved by the power of storytelling; real-life stories helped to move the dialogue from abstract doctrine to concrete practicalities. Information pamphlets distributed in Chile shared the experience of a representative woman, *Debora*, a poor pregnant Catholic who has decided to have an abortion but is overwrought with guilt. Through fictionalized narrative, Debora asks critical questions; most importantly, who has the moral authority to make decisions about her body and life? As a Catholic feminist, it was reassuring to Stephanie that neither the Bible nor Catholic teachings were rejected in the reframing of individual conscience within the Catholic faith. The non-judgmental voice that responds to Debora's questions does not provide the *right answer*, but rather, leaves room for Debora and the pamphlet's reader to develop the ability to ask the *right questions*.

And, though we rarely speak openly of this issue, domestic violence against women is an endemic and alarming issue in the West, even in a place like Canada that sees itself as progressive and egalitarian. Canada's Governor General, Michaelle Jean, recently spoke of this discomforting reality at a conference, *Communities Working to End Violence Against Women*, hosted in the province of Ontario: "Each of us, women and men, together in this room, believe profoundly that the right to be free and safe, free and safe at home, free and safe in your neighborhood, your community, is fundamental." Jean, who helped set up a network of emergency shelters in Quebec, worries that too often women's suffering in the West is kept *hidden behind closed doors, under a veil of shame and embarrassment*. "We don't see them, we don't hear them, but they are there, taking the full brunt of the abuse."

Alberta, the Canadian province where I live, has the highest levels of domestic violence in Canada. In 2004/2005, provincial women's shelters in Alberta accommodated 5,998 women and 5,488 children, but turned away another 5,150 women and their 3,710 children because they were full. Alberta is Canada's most economically prosperous province.

There is shame. Within our community, and within the lives of individual men and women, we hold this shameful secret tight to our vest. We squirm when someone asks about statistics or details. Each study's definition of violence is different; methodologies vary and include small sample sizes, a lack of control groups and weak assessment tools. Yet however defined—*murder, rape, marital rape, sexual assault, physical assault, emotional abuse, battering, stalking, prostitution, genital mutilation, sexual harassment, pornography*—the evidence is undeniable.

Twenty years of surveys in the United States by the National Research Council establishes that a woman who suffers violence is likely to know her assailant. In Canada, the Canadian Women's Foundation's *Shelter from the Storm* campaign jars our complacency with statistics reflecting back a culture of abuse: 51 percent of women in Canada have experienced at least one incident of physical or sexual violence since the age of sixteen and 61 percent of adults in Canada say they personally know at least one woman who has experienced physical or sexual abuse. If this were a contagious disease, we'd label it a pandemic.

Certainly, females do perpetrate violence against men, but with far less frequency and for different reasons. Experts who look at sexual symmetry in marital violence have data to support the differences. Husbands commonly hunt down and kill wives who have left them; husbands kill wives as part of planned murder-suicides; husbands kill wives who are unfaithful. Wives rarely respond in the same way, and in fact, spouse killings perpetrated by wives are often acts of self-defence.

This is awkward for Westerners. How could the horrors of physical rituals in the East even be mentioned in the same breath as violence against females in the privileged West? Unquestionably, we are chilled by stories of fathers in Afghanistan settling their loans—paying for their poppy production with drug traffickers—by selling their daughters. We shudder when mass media tells us that in poorer places, an opium bride is worth $3,000 US. And, the real-life experiences of people like Ayaan Hirsi Ali (who writes about her youth in Somalia in *Infidel*) and the firsthand stories shared by others—Khadija Al-Salami in *Tears of Sheba*, Azar Nafisi in *Reading Lolita in Tehran*, and Khaled Hosseini in *A Thousand Splendid Suns*—to name but a few, are raw. The West is a decent place by comparison, a place where women have legal rights.

And yet, violence against women endures.

In May 2008, I was invited to Calgary's "Inaugural Non-Gala in support of the Calgary Women's Emergency Shelter." Calgary's toniest gathered together in a downtown ballroom to publicly donate to the shelter: *Help Create a Teen Room for $10,000; Supply a baby crib and bedding for $500.* The well-heeled crowd unstintingly delivered, positioning the non-gala organizers to move forward in their vision of a well-appointed shelter for battered women in Calgary. Over the evening, I flinched in my chair sucking in air from time to time, trying to smile outwardly and come to grips with the unease in my gut. What was the matter with me: Wasn't this great—the "haves" stepping forward to support the "have-nots"? It is wonderful that Calgary can afford to build a bigger and better shelter for more and more battered women and their families; we have the good fortune of living in a community that can afford this shameful secret.

Why does violence against women happen in my hometown, and with such frequency? How could our community not allow women who were abused the breathing space to unload their shame-filled secret, to aright the tragic stigma? In *Women Who Run with the Wolves*, Clarissa Pinkola Estes warned us that the keeping of secrets cuts a woman off from those who would give her love and protection: *It causes her to carry the burden of grief and fear all by herself, and sometimes for an entire group, whether family or culture.*

In *Violence against Women*, editors Claire Renzetti and Raquel Kennedy Bergen share their dialogues with convicted rapists, a study conducted in the United States. Rapists want to "discipline and punish women", to "put them in their place" and thereby prove "manhood"; rapists assume that women both ask for and enjoy rape; rapists want impersonal sex so they don't have to please a female. Violence against women is higher in the United States than in most other Western countries, the authors report, partly because the American society is so materialistic and object-oriented. Treating women like objects is just an extension of this entitlement thought process.

What perverse cocktail of societal and individual attitudes allows aggressors to transform female human beings into objects? Some even *blame the females*. In Australia, the highest Muslim cleric, Sheikh Taj el-Din al-Hilali, gave a shocking Friday sermon in 2006 comparing uncovered women to meat left out for a cat to eat: *"If you take out uncovered meat and place it outside...and the cats come and eat it...whose fault is it, the cats' or the uncovered meat?"*

In *Reconciliation*, Benazir Bhutto seizes on Sheikh al-Hilali's argument as a violation of Islam. From both Islamic and Western perspectives, blaming the victim is inflammatory. Police, the justice system and health-care providers can be reluctant to intervene in family violence, but across the globe, these attitudes are shifting and East and West are converging in their expectations. Secrets are being shared.

East and West converge

Narrative storytelling can create the pause we need to see people as flesh and blood humans. Stories allow us to hear the concrete details of the choices individuals make in day-to-day living. The media attempts to share stories about gender dilemmas experienced in communities across the world—appalling stories about life under the burqa in Afghanistan is a contemporary theme—but the personalized stories of individual men and women are often lost in the drama of politics and war.

Consumer culture uses storytelling in the marketplace, but too often, as a way to reinforce negative messages. In communities around the world, adolescent girls hear the same story: *you are not pretty enough; you are not good enough; you are not thin enough.* The people in the advertising industry know that in order to sell things, they must convince girls and women that these things will add something to how they see themselves or are seen by others...you are not buying a product but an identity. This beauty myth is perplexing. Eternal beauty doesn't exist in nature, so how do we manage to equate beauty and goodness, ugliness and evil? Females' focus on aesthetic beauty can be all-consuming; women sometimes fear that they will lose their husband's affection after an operation. Men can seem incapable of loving a woman if she is ugly. Physical beauty fades and vigor diminishes as we age; the beauty myth and its obsession with externalities mangle our sense of worth and our identity.

In 2005, Bridges Social Development launched a program called *Through their Eyes* to encourage adolescent girls in Canadian and Yemeni communities to share their stories via videos. Professional journalists mentored these young girls in their story-telling debuts. Despite their many differences—the Canadian girls wore miniskirts and make-up instead of hijab—the stories unveiled the remarkable similarities as we got deeper into the *Gender Onions*. Girls in Yemen and Canada believe that gender equality is viable within their culture and faith depending on the choices they make; the girls share ambitious career goals; and all the storytellers look primarily to their parents and then teachers for role models.

Their stories also exposed common vulnerabilities. All the girls felt manipulated, at times, by the one-two punch of consumer culture and the media. Most of us know what it feels like to strive: wanting to be *attractive* to the other sex; trying to be *the good girl* or *the macho guy*. Sometimes we feel like we can never measure up to the expectations set by airbrushed models in magazines. Their shared *poke* at consumer culture's homogenization brought these young storytellers out of their isolation and hardened their resolve to expose the manipulation and confront the stereotypes. Local culture wasn't submerged in their stories, yet sisterhood became universal. The *Real Beauty* campaign launched by Dove soap— rejecting the normal trends in the beauty industry and using *real* women with a variety of ages, sizes and shapes as models—taps into this wisdom. Girls and women, everywhere, are weary of this focus on external beauty and want to identify with beauty within.

In Yemen, Bridges routinely invites female pioneers—the first female engineer, the first female news broadcaster, the first female surgeon—to tell their stories. These stories of courage and personal risk-taking shared by women on the front lines of change in their communities are gripping. Female judges from southern Yemen—a former British protectorate, then communist regime where women in law were commonplace—talk of the personal threats and intimidation they experienced with the re-unification of South Yemen and North Yemen in 1990. Everyone who listens sits, white-knuckled and anxious, on the edge of his or her seat.

One of my favorite female pioneers in Yemen is Dr Ahlam binBriek. The first time I met Ahlam, she introduced me to shy young girls in remote desert communities of the Hadhramout whom she had handpicked for midwife training. Recent International Labor Organization statistics for Yemen reinforce the compelling need to train doctors, nurses and midwives who can focus on women's health needs: 35 percent of Yemeni women do not receive health care; over 77 percent of babies are born at home; only 27 percent of deliveries are assisted by trained practitioners and postnatal care is provided to a mere 12 percent of mothers. *Inshallah—if Allah wills*—is frequently invoked, along with a resigned shrug, when people question Yemen's staggering maternal mortality rates.

Early marriage is a complicating factor. According to the United Nation's Child Rights Convention, early marriage is a marriage that takes place before the bride or groom reaches the age of eighteen. In Yemen, early marriage is common. Traditionalists defend the practice on the basis that if they marry their daughters off early, they can preserve their daughter's honor and that of the family. Yet, many question the practice: "One girl was 14 and got married. Now she has a son and she is still a child herself." In a 2008 report prepared by Save the Children Sweden in cooperation with the Gender-Development Research and Studies Center at Sana'a University, the report's research leader, Pernilla Ouis, identified a strong relationship between early marriage and increased domestic violence against girls, as well as an increase in the number of divorces among young couples. "Then you have poverty which is forcing families to marry off their daughters to alleviate financial burdens and expenses on education.... Because of the conditions that girls and young mothers face, Yemen is ranked at the very bottom of the Mother's Index 2007... Out of 33 least developed countries, Yemen is ranked 31."

For pioneers like Dr Ahlam, better training of female health-care providers—who in turn can enhance women's access to health care—is also *Allah's will*. But, I'm always nervous when others perceive the stories of Yemen's pioneers as *heroic*. Are these superhuman feats replicable?

In *The Wisdom of Crowds*, James Surowiecki cautions our tendency to treat corporate CEOs, athletes and entertainers as modern-day heroes. While impressive in his leadership, Lee Iacocca could not single-handedly save capitalism or Chrysler; the collective wisdom of an independent management team trumps that of even the smartest CEO. Likewise, U2's Bono and Oprah Winfrey cannot perform miracles in Africa; their RED campaign to fight HIV/Aids in Africa needs the commitment of thousands of consumers willing to purchase RED products for this cause.

When *hero* language starts to creep into someone's story, listen up. Many in the owning class exude confidence and like to be seen as the powerful hero. Middle-class heroes—including Gandhi—often feel guilty about the inequalities in the world and are highly motivated to push for social change. For them, the benevolent hero image is appealing—these individuals enjoy being the champion for others who are less fortunate. Bridges Social Development frequently sees people drawn to this role of defender of the underdog; Canadians are very prone to champion the little guy, even with our professional sports teams. Within Bridges' volunteer ranks, we have to unequivocally reinforce our objective: we're building human capacity in Yemen; we're not rescuing oppressed victims.

In Western-based stories about Muslim women, we often see the West portrayed as powerful or beneficial heroes dashing in to save oppressed victims. Casting a Muslim woman as a *victim* of oppression—or casting any woman as a victim, anywhere—does little to empower her. In a 2007 Academy of Management Review, researchers Robin Ely and Irene Padavic provocatively ask: *Is women's subordination a requirement for celebrating their worth?*

A 2006 cover of *Maclean's*, a Canadian magazine, was the trigger for me; it was a photo of a small girl, her eyes bare, standing almost crushed within a huddle of veiled women. Eyes huge, mouth down-turned, the symbolism screamed—*this is my future*. In the eyes of the Western world, the manner in which Muslim women dress means they are oppressed, have no say, have no power.

It can't be denied that the veil—in many ways—is symbolic of oppression, but it's not that simple. This focus on symbolic barriers obscures our view of the individuals beneath the veils; their hearts, their creativity, their passion. And has the potential to strip them of hope. Since change often happens first in the subtlest of human interaction, this may be a case where oppression could disappear at even more fundamental levels before the outward tradition of the veil disappears. *It may in fact be the last piece of the puzzle to fall in place, not the first.* And to myopically focus on veiling rather than taking action to make small but fundamental changes is consigning these women to the hopeless, and not helping Islamic-West interfacing or even the Muslim women themselves. And, these symbols are complicated. Ironically, Western-born Muslim girls are now choosing to wear a headscarf—the very same scarves that their mothers jettisoned on their arrival from Iran and Pakistan—as a liberating act of generational defiance.

In *Women Who Run with the Wolves*, Clarissa Pinkola Estes explores the symbolism of veiling. Putting a veil over something increases its action or feeling, suggests Estes: "Veiling the bowl" meant placing a white cloth over a bowl of kneaded dough to cause the bread to rise. "The veil for the bread and the veil for the psyche serve the same purpose. There is a potent leavening…a powerful fermenting going on. To be behind the veil increases one's mystical insight… In feminine psychology, the veil is a symbol for women's ability to take on whatever presence or essence they wish." Even fruit trees in blossom can be seen as wearing beautiful veils.

As usual, we've been busy obsessing about externalities—the physical veil—when it is the lifting of the inner veils that needs attention. Sufis speak of the seventy thousand veils of light and darkness that separate us from our real identity; to enter the Garden of Truth, we must learn to cast aside the veils:

> Seventy Thousand Veils separate Allah, the One Reality,
> from the world of matter and of sense.
> And every soul passes before his birth through these seventy thousand.
> The inner half of these are veils of light:
> the outer half, veils of darkness.

In his novel, *Till We Have Faces*, C.S. Lewis tells the story of Orual, a woman in search of her true face, her identity as a person. For most of her life, Orual wears a veil to cover the ugliness of her face and refuses to listen to her inner voice. She bitterly curses the gods who have caused her unhappiness. Orual cuts herself off from feminine influence and plunges into a masculine role. When, ultimately, she comes to know her own face, to appreciate her feminine individuality, she understands why the gods did not speak to her or answer her complaints: *How can they meet us face to face till we have faces?*

What does it take to be able to see our faces?

Complete honesty about our thoughts, feelings and actions. Our "faces" shine out from within.

To be in hell, Helen Luke suggests, is to refuse the tension of the opposites and therefore, all self-knowledge. "To be in purgatory is to accept that tension and to enter the long struggle for the knowledge of who we are, a struggle which involves the passionate integrity whereby we stand by our own truth even against the gods on whatever level of awareness we may be. We must accept every last shred of responsibility for our own story. There is no room for sitting on the fence. That is the only fatal flaw."

Are we capable of such utter honesty? As F. David Peat reminds us in *Pathways of Chance*, science and technologies are not going to save the world, neither are computer models and policy studies. Yet humans might: "Institutions may be the dinosaurs of the modern world, yet they are composed of human beings who think and feel and are born with the capacity for unlimited creativity." This may be our uniquely human capacity.

Moving forward

How, exactly, does the West see its role in this mythical quest for gender equality within communities dotted across the planet? It is a question that bears asking, repeatedly. Multilateral organizations—the United Nations and the World Bank—set the standards for equality, endorsing conventions and human rights principles which are then— *more or less*—voluntarily adopted by individual countries. The UN-championed Millennium Development Goals make unequivocal commitments to eliminate gender discrimination and empower women; improve maternal health and achieve universal primary education. The UN Convention on the Elimination of all Forms of Discrimination against Women—CEDAW—requires political leaders in endorsing countries to *pursue by all appropriate means and without delay a policy of eliminating discrimination against women by any person, organization or enterprise*, even to modify prejudicial social and cultural patterns that reinforce harmful stereotypes.

No small feat, yet this multilateral pull delivers results. The World Bank is crowing about the narrowing of the education gap between males and females. At the close of 2007, *The Economist* magazine reported that literacy rates among young women (aged 15 to 24) were higher than they were among young men in 54 of 123 countries: *Educationally, girls have long outperformed boys in rich countries. Now some poor countries are starting to reverse the male advantage.* This is all good, *The Economist* concludes: Female education is closely correlated with smaller family size and better educated women help countries move into higher-tech businesses, as is happening in India. In Canada, experts like Susan Pinker are even asking if male students are discriminated against in the classroom.

What, really, is our aspiration?

Aboriginals in Canada refer to the aim, not as gender equality, but as *gender balancing*. Aboriginal cultures also encourage decision-makers to take a longitudinal look—seven generations back and seven generations forward—to ensure that cumulative impact is understood.

In discussions with Islamic faith leaders in Yemen, the destination is *gender harmonization*. Dr Adel Mohammed Bahameed wears several hats: he was born in Seiyun, the heart of Yemen's Hadhramout region; trained as a medical doctor in Aden; married and has young children; acts as Executive Director of Al-Awn Foundation for Development; and is a frequent speaker in the mosque. In 2006, Dr Adel and I spent five hours in a 4x4 trek across the desert, driving from coastal Mulkulla to interior Seiyun. Most of our journey was spent discussing how to broach the topic of *gender equality* in Yemen. The term is offensive to many in Yemen—it is seen as a Western value associated with promiscuity and social problems ranging from latch-key kids to drug and alcohol abuse.

How could we reframe the issue to encourage dialogue in Yemen?

Through face-to-face engagement, Bridges' volunteers know that the Yemeni aspire to create an egalitarian society built on laws, human rights and economics—but also a society that enables feminine and masculine contribution in harmony with local culture and personal faith. Together, we have branded this process *gender jihad*: women and men struggling for equality in the home, workplace and state, and therefore, performing the most holy of causes. One of Bridges' local sponsors, Dr Abdul Karim Al-Eryiani, former Prime Minister in Yemen, assures those of us from the West that *gender jihad* is spiritually and culturally accurate. There is confusion in the West about the emotionally charged term *jihad*, Dr Eryiani explains: *"The word jihad does not really mean exclusively to fight—it means any effort performed in earnest towards the fulfilment of a noble goal."* So after much deliberation, we agreed to define the quest as *jihad al mawadah—the internal struggle for respectful, nurturing, loving and harmonious relationships between man and woman.*

Positioning and persistence are critical. How many people in African-American communities in the United States challenged racial discrimination before Rosa Parks refused to give up her seat on a city bus to a white passenger in December of 1955, sparking a massive civil rights campaign? How many suffragists in Canada sought political rights before Emily Murphy, Henrietta Muir Edwards, Louise McKinney, Irene Parlby and Nellie McClung—*The Famous 5*—launched the landmark *Persons' Case* which in 1929 declared women to be persons under Canadian law with the right to be appointed to the Senate of Canada? How many girls died from infections following unsafe female genital cutting before Egypt's politicians and faith leaders banned the practice?

It takes everything that I have learned to not turn Baby Ali and his mother into the *victims* and Bridges into the *hero* of this story. Yet, I know, it just wouldn't work. Even with a million volunteers in Yemen, Bridges cannot *fix* all the malnourished babies and their illiterate mothers.

Neither Bridges—nor any outsider—can unilaterally change values or practices within local communities, in Yemen or anywhere. But apathy isn't a moral option anymore. What we can do is provide support—*ideas, incentives, education, encouragement, training, mentorship, trust, respect*—to opinion leaders who are uniquely qualified to influence on-the-ground gender practices within their own communities. We can champion people like Dr Al-Kaff and Dr Ahlam.

We can tell their stories.

We are flowers blooming in the desert.

Putting virgin soil under cultivation initiates a breakdown of what may be called the "body" of the soil.

William A. Albrecht, *Physical, Chemical, Biological Changes in Soil Community: Man's role in changing the face of the earth*

He breaks the wilderness. He clears the land of trees, brush, weed. The land is brought under his control; he has turned waste into a garden. Into her soil he places his plow.... She opens her broad lap to him.... Her lap is fertile.

Susan Griffin, *Woman and Nature: The roaring inside her*

The Reformers banned...the cult of the Virgin Mary and the saints, and so took these images away. Christianity became more of a male world than ever. Not only did it deprive the Christian imagination of powerful images and myths and thus made it a cerebral, emotionally impoverished and narrowly masculine affair, on a more basic level the only important people and "gods" now were all men.

Karen Armstrong, *The Gospel According to Women*

Chapter 5

The Individual and Faith

Wonder Woman, featured on the cover of the first issue of *Ms.* Magazine in July 1972, became the patron saint of the feminist movement. This must be a high-water mark for secularism; a comic book superhero held up as the icon of the ideal female. In the words of Gloria Steinem, Wonder Woman is a *symbol of strength, self-reliance for women, sisterhood and mutual support among women.* Others agree, including the Right Revd John Shelby Spong, retired bishop of the Episcopal Diocese of Newark: *Wonder Woman has done more to break the culturally imposed boundaries on women than the Virgin Mary ever did.*

Wonder Woman as our symbol of the sacred feminine; is this the enduring legacy of 1960s-style Western feminism? I've pulled on the Lycra bodysuit and didn't like the tight squeeze. And, I certainly wouldn't recommend the superwoman role model to Muslim friends. Of course, we crave an icon; we need the symbols, the images, even the mysticism of a sacred feminine. But, *Wonder Woman?*

Origins

As we saw in chapter three, there is much archaeological evidence that in early history both men and women worshipped goddesses, women functioned as priests, and property commonly passed through the mother's lineage. In *The Alphabet versus the Goddess*, Leonard Shlain provocatively asks, "What event in human history could have been so pervasive and immense that it literally changed the sex of God?"

Patriarchal religions are largely blamed for instituting a social order oppressive to women and nature, or at least are credited with sealing the victory for the patriarchy. Yet even as early as the fourth century BC, Aristotle judged females the weaker sex: "The male is by nature superior, and the female inferior; and the one rules and the other is ruled." In Greek mythology, the first woman, *Pandora*, is created as a punishment to men.

Feminism and religion have long been at loggerheads. Our scrutiny of Islam's treatment of women may be contemporary, but the issue isn't new for organized religion. In the early stages of the feminist movement, Elizabeth Cady Stanton pointed a gloved finger at Christianity: "The Bible and the church have been the greatest stumbling blocks in the way of woman's emancipation." Desmond Tutu, Nobel Peace Prize recipient and spiritual leader of the Anglican Church in South Africa, connects the dots between racial apartheid and gender apartheid: "For a long time in our church, we didn't ordain women, and we were penalizing a huge section of humanity for something about which they could do nothing— their gender... I'm glad that apartheid [gender apartheid] has ended."

Bishop Spong cuts even deeper, alleging that the Virgin Mary is a construct of a male world: "The patriarchal man wants purity in his wife, as well as a mother for his children. The Virgin Mother filled that need, but she was hardly an ideal woman. What man wants to be married to a permanent virgin? We need to remember that the world that proclaimed the Virgin Mary to be the ideal woman treated all women as second class citizens." It is hardly surprising that many seek to reinstate values embodied in a goddess religion, to recognize women's bodies as microcosms of the universe and honor women and nature as sacred.

Judaism, Christianity, Islam

To reiterate: the three major religions that were to so impact the world—Judaism, Christianity and Islam—did so with the advent of the written word, and subsequent control over who had access to it.

When you read the Bible, Jesus seemed to prefer to speak in symbols and parables. Socrates didn't commit his ideas to paper; he was convinced that face-to-face dialogue was the best path to wisdom. Buddha wrote nothing down; neither did Pythagoras, and all three, like Jesus, believed in equality between the sexes. Later, when others wrote linear words down, there is evidence they changed dramatically the things these teachers said.

Why, I have to ask myself, did the most profound teachers in history choose not to write down their words themselves? Could it be because they understood how the written word could be manipulated, and preferred their actions to speak?

According to Schlain, authoritarian leaders rely on the power of the written word, logos, and sometimes even *the word*, to classify people and ideas. We inherit this tradition of single file logic from the Greeks. Hebrews were the first to embrace alphabetic writing, and according to Schlain, alphabetic literacy enhanced their authority to enforce *the* word: "(Hebrew) Prophets accomplished these tasks without an army, police force, or sanctions—they managed to keep their young nation on the straight and narrow using exhortation alone because they could speak with authority about the principles set forth in a book that had *been written by God.*"

A culture that elevates the written word often does so at the expense of images. Which does appeal to different thought processes.

Whether or not Schlain is right about the *gender differences* in processing the written word, it is clear that patriarchy increased by use and misuse of it.

As a believer in God and a flesh and blood mother, I need to get behind the frontlines of this battlefield; Bishop Spong's notion of patriarchy going to the extreme measure of portraying the ideal woman as "sweet, passive, docile, compliant, obedient, virginal, and unreal" is hardly inspiring. And, deigning Mary a vessel for God (a male deity) to virginally implant Jesus (another male deity) without Mary having any role except as the container is an abrupt end to the female fertility mythology.

And, as the mother of sons, I must acknowledge that males were banished from the garden as well. In *The Myth of Matriarchal Prehistory*, Cynthia Eller reminds me: "No longer the cherished sons of the goddess, men are subject to cruel hierarchies of status among themselves, alienation from women and nature, and a painfully limited range of role choices."

Standing in the crossfire of my belief in equality and my belief in God sometimes doesn't allow much room to manoeuvre. Yet what coincidence. Here I am posing this critical question in the heartland of Islam—a female, a Christian—nearly within sight of the Sinai where Yahweh gave Moses the Ten Commandments.

My question is simple: if the goal of organized religion is to call all people into the fullness of their humanity—to restore dynamic equilibrium between the masculine and feminine within individuals—then why am I struggling to reconcile my vision of the soaring two-wingèd bird with gender hierarchies seemingly endorsed by faith? The best way for me to get answers to these questions is to look into the eyes of spiritual leaders I trust, and pose the questions, face to face.

So, that's what I did.

In Yemen, and in Canada, I asked faith leaders from a wide cross-section of Christian and Muslim denominations to explain to me how religion can reconcile our same source origin, our *oneness*, with male/female hierarchies that seem to have a firm footing in organized religion. Please, enlighten me, how did we get from *one source* to *patriarchy*?

In Yemen, consultations with Muslim leaders were not as intimidating as one might expect. The reflections of a Sufi imam from a very conservative community in the deserts of the Hadhramout were particularly illuminating. Through a bit of divine intervention or synchronicity or luck—however you describe critically important meetings that materialize without a logical plan—I was able to spend time with Omar Bin Mohammed Bin Salem Bin Hafeedh, a Sufi imam who together with his brother runs a boarding school, or *madrassa*, in Tarim, Yemen.

Decked out in a newly-purchased black abaya, a black headscarf hastily drawn to restrain my unruly blonde hair, I kneeled down across from this esteemed imam who was sitting cross-legged on a Persian-style carpet, dressed in an Omani-style headscarf, his eyes tired yet twinkling behind the Coke-bottle thick lenses of dark-rimmed eyeglasses. I leaned forward. *I'm always on the lookout for the signs of God in the eyes of spiritual leaders.* Imam Omar, together with the English speakers among his disciples, treated us to ubiquitous Yemeni hospitality: the creamiest halwa sweets I've ever tasted and freshly-picked dates, downed with cups of spicy Yemeni coffee brewed from the ground husks of coffee beans boiled in water and sweetened with heaps of sugar. Amin, an Islamic convert from England, acted as translator; his gentle demeanor enabled unstilted dialogue. Everyone at the madrassa put their hand over their heart to signal the beginning of the formal exchange; I mirrored the sentiment. Invoking love, and God, into this conversation seemed like a very good idea.

After commenting on my intrepidness, Imam Omar launched into the heart of the matter. Relying on the Qur'an to reinforce his opinion, he described how the origins of masculine and feminine in the worldly realm came from *one* source, a single soul. Within Islam, gender issues were misunderstood and exploited: "Misunderstandings create vulnerabilities that can be exploited to divide people; misunderstandings create different levels of humans, hierarchies and differences that are incompatible with the one source."

This sounded reassuringly familiar; this was the elusive *voice of moderate Islam* that I strained to hear in the West. What courage: It was one thing for me, a citizen of a liberal country to be critical of fundamentalist religion; here was a faith leader from within the heartland of Islamic fundamentalism explaining to me how religion has been used to polarize women against men, and more importantly, women against women.

Back in Canada, I gathered around Christian and Islamic faith leaders for the same conversation. The Islamists concurred with the Yemeni faith leaders: we are created from a single soul, thus *rights* between males and females are not different. But, there was a catch: *roles* can be differentiated based on physical attributes of men and women. The *biology is our destiny* theory was given a sound thrashing based on a rereading of Genesis 1 and 2 from the Bible. There was sensitivity; a few of the non-evangelical Protestants were uncomfortable assigning sex-based roles. Oh no... dialogue was on the brink of descending into the abyss of polarizing doctrine!

Then, an epiphany: the Revd Clint Mooney, a United Church pastor originally from the Maritimes region of Canada provocatively asked: "Is stronger/weaker really the right dichotomy; in fact, is equality between genders really the right question?"

According to his interpretation of Genesis 2, God created an androgynous being—neither male nor female—and from this genderless being, God created a system of male-female pairing in humans and in animals. This interpretation parallels several verses of the Qur'an that state that God created man and woman from a single life-cell or being. In my Sufi guidebook, *The Garden of Truth*, Seyyed Hossein Nasr describes sexual union as an earthly reflection of a paradise prototype: "The male experiences the Infinite and the female the Absolute in this earthly union, which returns, albeit for a moment, the human being to his or her androgynic wholeness."

Revd Mooney's conclusion? Humans have a need to come back to this original state of one-ness. As a female, I can't experience the whole expanse of worldview without experiencing maleness; ditto for males. Biologically this resonates; there has to be male and female cooperation for the species to endure. In the secular realm, this *two become one* concept echoes the language of marriage. By partnering, the combined masculine-feminine worldview of my husband and I is more expansive, even creating the potential to be whole.

This explanation is inviting; diffusing the tension and friction and fighting between feminine and masculine is an appealing aim.

And there is reconciliation with Islam. The Qur'an states:

O people! Be careful of (your duty to) your Lord, Who created you from a single being and created its mate of the same (kind) and spread from these two, many men and women; and be careful of (your duty to) Allah, by Whom you demand one of another (your rights), and (to) the ties of relationship; surely Allah ever watches over you.

(Yet, I am nervous too. By combining the *two-ness* of maleness and femaleness into the *one-ness* of a couple, we need to be on guard; individuals must recognize and accept each other's individual wholeness. We can't compromise Osho's vision of man and woman as independent yet interdependent: *And the oak tree and the cypress grow not in each other's shadow.* I find myself squirming a bit too, thinking about what this means for people who don't choose to partner, or for homosexuality; the diminished potential for an expansive worldview.)

After some reflection, our group reverted to the familiar terrain of who to blame: Was it patronizing to women for male faith leaders—in Catholicism, Islam or any organized faith—to *permit* females' voices to be heard, if not from the pulpit but from the pew? Was it patronizing *to men* to conclude that a woman as faith leader presented irresistible temptation? The Yemeni have no trouble acknowledging that a woman's beauty can arouse sexual desire in men; why are we surprised that a lack of female modesty naturally leads to sexual harassment or rape? In the "Welcome to Yemen" tourist brochure handed out to visitors by Yemen's Cultural Center for Foreigners, veiling is explained: *The motivation of [rape] is the attractive beauty of women and showing off their bodies. So the veil is a means of protection for a woman to avoid harm to her.* How on Earth did sex become such a weapon between men and women; a point of control rather than an incentive to harmonization? The sad truth is that sex is power, sometimes the only power card that women hold in their hands.

Encouraging modesty and seclusion for the female temptress is not exclusively Islamic; recall the words of Paul in the New Testament of the Christian Bible:

But I would have you know, that the head of every man is Christ; and the head of the woman is the man; and the head of Christ is God. Every man praying or prophesying, having his head covered, dishonoreth his head. But every woman that prayeth or prophesieth with her head uncovered dishonoreth her head: for that is even all one as if she were shaven. For if the woman be not covered, let her also be shorn: but if it be a shame for a woman to be shorn or shaven, let her be covered. For a man indeed ought

Donna Kennedy-Glans with her husband, Laurie Glans, and three sons
in Canmore, Alberta

Donna Kennedy-Glans in front of the Aga Sophia in Istanbul, Turkey

Traditional health-care leaders in Socotra, Yemen, meeting with the Minister of Public Health and Population. "Solutions to seemingly intractable gender integrity dilemmas are possible when a whole group of engaged individuals and organizations agree to do something differently."

Dr Al-Kaff with a Bridges' volunteer midwife in Tarim, Yemen

Bedouin mother, Mulkulla, Yemen

Bedouin newborn, Wadi Hadhramout, Yemen

Young boys dressed for Friday prayers,
Shibam, Hadhramout, Yemen

Young girls playing soccer, Jibbla,
Yemen

Bridges' youth training in Sana'a, Yemen

Yemeni family photo,
Sana'a Yemen

Camel-driven grinder in Bab-el-Yemen
marketplace in Sana'a Yemen

Young girls in Aden, Yemen

Wadi Do'an, Yemen [Patrick McCloskey]

Ancient terracing in Yemen [Patrick McCloskey]

Young girl in Yemeni highlands
carrying washing bucket
[Patrick McCloskey]

Yemeni women climbing stairs to water well
[Patrick McCloskey]

Young Yemeni girl with donkey hauling water up the steep hills
of Wadi Do'an [Patrick McCloskey]

Photo by Walid Rubaih,
World Friends, Sana'a,
Yemen circa 1930

I was called *labbeh tyur* in Arabic: Bird Necklace.

I was crafted by Jewish silversmiths living in the Yemen's capital of Sana'a in the 1930s, before the Jewish exodus to Israel. Incredibly, Muslims attributed special magic powers to me—*baraka* or sacred otherness—because I was crafted by foreigners, in this case, Yemenite Jews. An amulet: I protect brides on their wedding days, against evil and disease, and invite fertility.

Is it not remarkable that my value as talisman overruled Judeo-Islamic written taboos about figurative representation and crossed over religious boundaries?

Can you not see the delicate gilt-silver filigree motifs; birds, hearts, little hands and leaves, bowknots, bells, tiny stars and crescent moons?

Baraka—said to be my witchcraft in reverse—floats between its parts, at times even disrupting unyielding authority, entrenched ideas of what is right and what is wrong.

I create breathing space.

I represent hope.

Flowers are blooming in the deserts of Yemen

not to cover his head, forasmuch as he is the image and glory of God: but the woman is the glory of the man. For the man is not of the woman; but the woman of the man. Neither was the man created for the woman; but the woman for the man.

THE HOLY BIBLE: I CORINTHIANS 11:3-9

Quest

Given the influence of the temple, the church, the cathedral and the mosque on the question of male and female rights and roles, the values of this monotheistic trio of believers—*Jews, Christians, and Muslims*—is the focus of my scrutiny. There is much debate, but justification for female subordination and male authority has been endorsed within the Jewish, Christian and Islamic faiths on the basis of three assumptions:

First, God's primary creation is man, not woman; woman is created from man's rib, hence is derivative;

Second, woman was the primary agent of *The Fall*, man's expulsion from the Garden of Eden, thus *all daughters of Eve* should be suspected as temptresses; and

Third, woman was created not only *from* man but *for* man, which makes female existence instrumental not fundamental.

Who has the authority to interpret deeply rooted, spiritually based doctrine on the rights and roles of men and women? If religious truth derives from revelation, then reason and even deliberation can be suspended. Without dialogue to rigorously test the truth of beliefs, how can the faithful risk the hazards posed by gaps between the secular and the sacred? Imagine the anxiety: a Catholic mother in a high-risk pregnancy has the legal option to choose abortion, but not the moral choice; a Muslim father of a teenage daughter living in North America is guided by faith to ask his daughter to wear a face veil, but locals condemn the practice.

Religious zealots interpret their religious belief in the language of absolutes. Right to life advocates who kill doctors performing abortions obscure the division of the world of God and the world of man, infusing worldly struggles with divine meaning. Islamic extremists who commit acts of terrorism—killing women who refuse to wear hijab—justify their actions based on their belief in a higher moral purpose. Millions of Christians denounce abortion, but they don't pick up a gun and kill abortion doctors. Likewise, millions of Muslims endorse modest dress for women but do not kill women who choose to not veil. Radical fundamentalists buttress the walls that close in and divide us, walls between men and women, and even more callously, walls between women and women.

Conversation is the bonding force between men and women—Margaret Atwood's invisible *third hand*. Can we extend the image to include conversation that allows the secular and the spiritual paths to dynamically reconcile and coexist?

> (The man and the woman walk down the street,
> hand in passionate hand; but whose hand is it really?
> It's the third hand each one holds, not the beloved's.
> It's the third hand that joins them together,
> the third hand that keeps them apart.)

Vertical and lateral dialogue can open up a continuum of options. Yet, what, exactly, is *dialogue*? We talk about *dialogue* a lot, yet rarely agree on its meaning. In an October 2008 report, "Changing Course: A New Direction for US Relations with the Muslim World," produced by thirty-four Americans from religious, business, military, foreign affairs, academic, and not-for-profit circles (including Muslim Americans; Madeleine Albright, former US secretary of state; former US president Bill Clinton, and two former Republican congressmen), this leading citizen coalition recommended America's acceleration of diplomacy as the *primary* tool of global engagement and *face-to-face* relationships to better learn about one another's nation and culture.

Historic dialogue has also taken place in the last few years between Vatican officials and the coalition of 138 Muslim authors of the open letter "A Common Word between Us and You" addressed to the Pope and other Christian leaders in October 2007 for the purpose of establishing a World Muslim-Catholic Forum; the Sufi imam I met in Tarim, Yemen is one of those 138 Muslim authors. The ground rules for *dialogue* at this historic meeting have been established:

> Dialogue is by definition between people of different views, not people of the same views. Dialogue is not about imposing one's views on the other side, nor deciding oneself what the other side is and is not capable of, not even of what the other side believes. Dialogue starts with an open hand and an open heart. It proposes but does not set an agenda unilaterally. It is about listening to the other side, as it speaks freely for itself, as well as about expressing one's own self. Its purpose is to see where there is common

ground in order to meet there and thereby make the world better, more peaceful, more harmonious and more loving.

My quest to understand the *sacred feminine* isn't an admission that secularism has failed. It is an admission that our values on gender do not derive exclusively from economic, legal, corporate or political authority. Modernization and globalization haven't extinguished values and images— including eternal beliefs about the feminine and the masculine—closely guarded by cultural and spiritual communities. Millions of people in the world, including Muslims and Orthodox Jews, believe that God revealed law governing the whole of human affairs. For Muslims, the Shari'a is intended to cover life in its entirety, not some arbitrarily demarcated private sphere. A secular path remains critical to restoration of dynamic equilibrium between male and female, but it has run a parallel path to the spiritual realm. Since 9/11, these separated paths—secular and spiritual— have had no choice but to relate to one another, either as competitors trying to convert each other, or in cooperation. This is yet another vital opening, maybe even the most significant since the separation of Church and State by many Western nations. Present circumstances free the secular world to take a poke at legalistic, overly politicized, and spiritually poor distortions of religion.

Our experience with secularism in the West demonstrates to non-secular societies how politics, economics, law and the private sector positively—or negatively—influence relations between males and females. Secularism isn't a panacea. We still have a lot of unanswered questions: Is our lay vision one of a gender-neutral society—*a level playing field*— where no allowances are made for differences between men and women? Wise thinkers and biologists keep reminding me: an *exhale* and an *inhale* are necessary for breathing, but one is not the same as the other. In an increasingly globalized world where everything and everyone becomes a commodity, is it our intention or an unforeseen consequence of our secular tactics to, in effect, reward females—*Wonder Women*—who adopt competitive, masculine traits? Looks like homogenization run amok. Secularism really can struggle to put a non-financial value on feminine (as distinguished from female) contribution to society.

But, I repeat, this is not a failure of secularism.

Most Westerners are wary of looking at gender equality through a spiritual lens. We spent centuries separating Church and State, creating progressive modern societies that allow for unassailable human rights. It isn't surprising that, until now, the modern women's movement has been secular. Some fear a revival of religion: In his book, *Secularism Confronts*

Islam, Olivier Roy examines secularism in France, and contends: "(the) problem is not Islam but religion or, rather, the contemporary forms of the revival of religion."

Roy is right; a new breed of charismatic faithful is reasserting their spiritual values, and naturally, there is nervousness about whether believers can bring spirituality and culture into political realms without trying to impose their values and traditions on others.

Since September 11, the walls between faiths have grown higher and thicker. Policy Director for Cultural Issues with Concerned Women for America warns of the danger of listening to false gospels and becoming secularized: "We're witnessing a growing trend within certain liberal sects of Christendom wherein leftist church leaders are pushing new-age, Bible-à-la-carte spiritualism. The mindset is, 'If God's Word doesn't comport with my view on morality, then I'm right and God is wrong…'." To reinforce this viewpoint, others point to the Bible:

> For the time will come when they will not endure sound doctrine; but wanting to have their ears tickled, they will accumulate for themselves teachers in accordance to their own desires; and will turn away their ears from the truth, and will turn aside to myths.

THE HOLY BIBLE, 2 TIMOTHY 4:3-4

It takes monumental effort to hold the dynamic tension between the secular and spiritual—permitting these values to coexist in a way that fosters the continuum of choices we need to be able to restore equilibrium between maleness and femaleness.

Reconciling faith

In 1985, the Tandem Project was initiated within the United Nations to find ways to hold individual religion or belief *in tandem* with the right of others to believe as they choose. More than two decades later, we are still grappling with the question, but the stakes are now much higher. In Canada, a stronghold of multiculturalism, we question the doctrine that preaches *tolerance* toward imported culture when that culture is fundamentally intolerant of women. What does *reasonable accommodation* mean for Canadians? Certainly, we can allow turbans for Sikhs who serve in the Royal Canadian Mounted Police and sport-style headscarves for Muslim girls who want to play soccer. But, what about polygamy, or stoning of adulteresses; when does *vive la différence* become unbearable?

The challenge with *reasonable* accommodation is that everyone has their own sense of what is reasonable; and who really gets to decide what is reasonable, the host or the outsider? Before meeting with the imam in Tarim, Yemen, it seemed uncomplicated to pull on an abaya and a scarf for the meeting; this voluntary act was intended to signal respect to my host, a small inconvenience in the pursuit of truth. When I was invited into Iran to work in 2003, I wore a long black skirt, a loose-fitting, long-sleeved, high-collared black suit jacket, black sandals and a scarf around my hair. I thought I was covered; the only skin that showed was my face, my hands and my toes. On arrival in Tehran, I realized to my horror that my toenails were painted bright red. Seeing these red toenails peeking out the ends of my black sandals made me panicked enough to rush out and purchase thick black stockings to wear with my sandals. I was genuinely afraid of being switched by the Iranian religious police, or worse. Feeling fear made me surprisingly outraged; as an outsider and non-Muslim, why were ultra-conservative Iranian religious rules being imposed on me?

Candid exploration of existential questions is surprisingly robust, not only in Yemen, but in every other Islamic country I've travelled to since September 11 where moderate Muslims are attempting to reconcile faith and the rights of males and females. Our sometimes stilted Western discourse on the more personal questions at the core of the *Gender Onion* can seem impoverished by contrast. Despite the cynicism in CNN's politicized storylines, nuances of culture and faith are being unravelled. What does the Qur'an say about the appointment of women as judges; about the responsibility of women as health-care providers; about the role of women in business; about domestic violence; about female circumcision? Patriarchal practices that compromise Qur'anic interpretations of the rights of women—honor killings, or arranged marriages that deny the need for female consent—are being openly debated. This renewal or renovation of Islam—an Islam gentler in its treatment of women—allows believers to speak from within their faith community. Some conservatives within Islam will continue to argue that religious doctrines are incompatible with human rights, particularly women's rights. Others will see the value of adaptation. Reformists will disentangle faith from patriarchal cultural practices. The dialogue can have more impact than the laws that spark the conversation. And, the dialogue is critical.

Riffat Hassan, a self-described Muslim, theologian and women's rights activist, believes that the dominant, patriarchal interpretations of Islam have fostered the myth of women's inferiority by taking Qur'anic verses out of context and reading them literally, ignoring the fact that the Qur'an often uses symbolic language to portray deep truths. The Hadith literature has been the lens through which the Qur'an has been interpreted through the ages, Hassan asserts: "reflecting the culture of the seventh- and eighth-century Arab world, the sayings voice the cumulative biases, against women, of the Jewish, Christian, Hellenistic, and pre-Islamic Bedouin Arab traditions."

Likewise, while some Christians believe the Bible is the literal *God-breathed* word of the Lord; others interpret the Bible as a *man-breathed* interpretation of God's word. Hassan focuses on two liberating themes within Islam: the fundamental equality of humans before God, and Islam's revolutionary aim of liberation, to encourage a reinterpretation of certain Qur'anic verses and Hadith that have been used against women:

Never will I suffer to be lost
The work of any of you,
Be he male or female:
Ye are members, one of another.

SURAH 3: AL-'IMRAN: 195

Yemen's Government knows that resistance to women's economic and political emancipation hinders its progress. As a poorer yet very endearing country in an affluent and conservative neighborhood, the country can't afford to ignore economics. Girls' education has been encouraged; gender equality laws have been passed; quotas for females in politics are being set. To support Yemen's Government and its citizens through this transition, Bridges' volunteers from Canada journey to Yemen to share know-how with their local counterparts. Learning has been reciprocal. Universally, the struggle for harmony between males and females—*gender jihad*—is a noble aspiration.

Tariq Ramadan, a Swiss-born academic and prolific writer on Islam, echoes the importance of this return to the *greater jihad*—(again, the spiritual struggle against one's ego as distinct from the *lesser jihad* of war against Islam's external enemies).

I am inspired by the ability of my counterparts in Yemen to draw on their faith as a source of support—and not an obstacle—in their pursuit of more balanced gender contribution in society. At a recent meeting of Bridges, Yemeni students in Canada earnestly expressed this desire—faith as a positive tool for change.

The Government of Yemen has extended secular rights to its citizens. People like Dr Ahlam binBriek of Mulkulla have reached out to accept this proffered secular baton in their one hand, but they haven't veered from the spiritual path. Despite the temptation to accelerate women's rights along a secular superhighway, Ahlam will not be forced to decide between feminism and her faith. *The women's rights movement in Yemen— and elsewhere in the Muslim world—is not an exclusively secular movement.* Ahlam is ruthlessly compassionate; relying on the Qur'anic idea that justice cares about the unequal conditions of different groups of people, she champions the well-being of the downtrodden, oppressed and the weak. Riffat Hassan explains that this idea of justice stems from the Qur'anic ideal of community, or *ummah*, a word derived from the root *umm*, meaning mother. Ahlam is an exemplary mother to her community, and can authoritatively point to the Qur'an as the foundation of her mandate.

I am also mobilized by the vision of *feminine jihad* as a peaceful counterbalance to the bloodshed of *fundamentalist jihad*.

Although many see September 2001 as the triggering event that refocused our attention on gender fundamentals within Islam, many snowballing events—including the declaration of communism in the far-flung reaches of Afghanistan—built momentum. Communist manifestos declared men and women equal. For tribal villages in Afghanistan comfortable with the segregation of the sexes, the egalitarian values endorsed by communism were shocking. It was an insult to centuries-old traditions to be told by a new government that their daughters had to leave home, attend school and work alongside men. The Taliban ruled most of Afghanistan from 1996 to 2001, and reacted by imposing an ultra-puritanical interpretation of Shari'a law. The Taliban's official policy was discrimination against women.

As Khaled Hosseini poignantly relates in *A Thousand Splendid Suns*, the Taliban's edicts for women were cruelly enforced by the Taliban's Ministry for Propagation of Virtue and Suppression of Vice, also known as the religious police:

> Attention women:
> You will stay inside your homes at all times. It is not proper for women
> to wander aimlessly about the streets. If you go outside, you must be
> accompanied by a mahram, a male relative. If you are caught alone on the
> street, you will be beaten and sent home.
> You will not, under any circumstance, show your face. You will cover with
> burqa when outside. If you do not, you will be severely beaten.
> Cosmetics are forbidden.
> Jewelry is forbidden.
> You will not wear charming clothes.

You will not speak unless spoken to.
You will not make eye contact with men.
You will not laugh in public. If you do, you will be beaten.
You will not paint your nails. If you do, you will lose a finger.
Girls are forbidden from attending school. All schools for girls will be closed immediately.
Women are forbidden from working.
If you are found guilty of adultery, you will be stoned to death.

The world rallied to the defence of Afghani women and girls; armed forces from several countries remain in Afghanistan to restrain the Taliban's reach. Women4Women in Afghanistan—and other Western-based advocates—raise millions of dollars to fund girls' education. Unveiling human potential in the remotest villages of Afghanistan has become a universal cause, talked about by families at kitchen tables around the globe. The Taliban continues to claim legitimacy; after being invited to take a role in the peace process by President Hamid Karzai, the Taliban released a shadow Afghan constitution that envisages a country where women would remain veiled and under-educated.

Tiny steps forward, but the burqa has not yet been fully lifted. As long as the endorsement of ultra-conservative clerics is seen as essential to survival by political incumbents in Afghanistan, backsliding on women's rights remains a constant threat.

The intersection of fundamentalism and a globalizing economy has given followers of Islam—indeed, all of us—a unique moment in history. This is not just something happening *over there*. The oppression of females we observe in Iran and Saudi Arabia—how can anyone ever justify floggings for rape victims or stoning of adulteresses—is forcing us out of our lethargy. South Africans woke up one day to find that the rest of the world didn't like them, didn't like racial apartheid; regimes that oppress females may soon be surprised to find the rest of the world equally repulsed by *gender apartheid*. Is gender discrimination any less appalling than racial discrimination?

This isn't just about Islam. Conservatives from all faiths have been critical of the *excesses* of feminism. The religious revival presently unfolding across the globe is forcing us to ask questions about the role of faith in the public sphere. The voice of organized religion is powerful—it always has been—but why do we keep turning a blind eye when faith and feminism square off; why does religion always seem to trump equality regardless of the form of government under which they reside?

Choices

The choices we make are critical.

In *The Upside of Down*, Thomas Homer-Dixon refers to these rarefied times as *moments of contingency*...a moment of choice, like the fork in the pathway encountered by the traveller in Robert Frost's poem "The Road Not Taken." Care must be taken in these moments, Homer-Dixon cautions, as surprise and bewilderment create mental polarities: "And, these polarities evoke the best and worst attributes of human character— courage and cowardice, generosity and greed, kindness and malice, and integrity and deceit."

Some have chosen to slam the door on constructive conversation about the rights and roles of men and women within organized religion. In her 2007 bestseller, *Infidel*, Ayaan Hirsi Ali writes about her youth in Somalia, Saudi Arabia, Ethiopia and Kenya, and about her freedom in the Netherlands. Hirsi Ali's personal story is painful, and in her bitterness, she condemns Islam for her suffering. In a powerful statement on Al Jazeera television, Wafa Sultan, an Arab-American psychologist from Los Angeles also criticizes Islam's backwardness in its treatment of women and reproaches the faith for its willingness to violate human rights to achieve religious ends. While Sultan endorses the right of individuals to believe as they choose, she has chosen secularism in lieu of organized religion. It was an *either-or* decision for Sultan. In *The End of Faith*, the *New York Times* bestseller, atheist Sam Harris goes even further to argue that in the presence of weapons of mass destruction, the encroachment of organized religion into world politics is lethal. To save civilization at this crossroads of militant Islam and the American religious right, Harris recommends that governments end their theological neutrality and oppose the toleration of religious beliefs of citizens. Anticipating dissent, Harris disparagingly asserts that "*the religious moderate is nothing more than a failed fundamentalist* whose tolerance and politeness stands in the way of their proclamation that *the Bible and the Koran both contain mountains of life-destroying gibberish.*"

At this fork in the gender pathway, we all have to consider our personal continuum of options and choose our path carefully. How exactly am I reconciling my faith and feminism? I was raised as a Presbyterian, a Christian denomination that invites men and women to the pulpit and is comfortable with culturally refreshed interpretations of Paul's preaching. When I married and moved away from my rural roots, I was invited to join a synod of the Lutheran church where my husband and extended family worshipped. The unflappable pastor of this traditional synod painstakingly explained their faith's theological rationale for excluding women from the pulpit, from voting and even from teaching adults. I was horrified by the sexism; there was no question that religion trumped rights in this Protestant congregation. After much conversation, I joined the church and immediately embarked on advocacy for change from within. Thankfully, some adjustments were made but women remain excluded from the pulpit and *Focus on the Family* role modelling continues to irritate. The masculine impression set by Luther and then Calvin is indelible.

As a female within a traditional Lutheran synod that defines the roles of men and women quite differently, my spectrum of options looks like this: If I wish to passively accept the faith's values on roles for men and women—a choice that will keep peace in my extended family—I can worship with this congregation and simply ignore the church's messages on gender. Alas, though, compartmentalization doesn't work for me, so ultimately, this option will also never work for me. Bitterness would be predictable. The value of equality is part of my essence and to deny or subordinate its worth would be the same as denying me oxygen.

I could adopt a constructive engagement strategy; remaining in this church and working from the inside to make changes. For the last two decades, this has been my choice. It is the same strategy that I adopted as a female executive in an oil company; obviously a comfort zone. Post September 11, I've struggled more and more with this option. The rising power of religion, everywhere, makes me nervous; it has seemed to close in the walls that the Lutheran faith has constructed to demarcate and protect its beliefs. I wholeheartedly participate in ecumenical discussions with other Christians, with Muslims and with other faiths but my own church discourages my reach outside the faith's boundaries. Their fear of apostasy is greater than the perceived fruit of dialogue. I shudder to think how daunting constructive engagement—working from within—must be for a man or woman belonging to a fundamentalist religion. In ultra conservative Islamic countries, like Afghanistan, the penalty for apostasy under Shari'a law is death.

Another option would be to remain within the Christian faith, but choose a more liberal denomination. As my box squeezes tighter, this option grows more compelling. Other options include the rejection of most organized religion, while preserving my own spirituality.

Unlike Harris, I could never reject faith.

One of my most daunting encounters with fundamentalist Islam took place in June 2006, at an all-girls school in Ta'iz—a poor and conservative Muslim city in the terraced highlands of Yemen. As executive director of Bridges Social Development I was overseeing a program to teach young girls how to tell their stories, how to define what is possible in their lives.

One critical partner in this work was Amat, the principal of this all-girls school. Amat is one of Ta'iz's first elected female politicians; her gentle brand of leadership has enabled her to deftly model feasible roles for women in this community in a non-threatening way.

Not surprisingly, many of Amat's fellow teachers at this all-girls school were anxious to understand Bridges' program, and our motivators: why did Canadians care about young girls in Yemen, were we trying to "westernize" their girls? A fellow volunteer and I were invited to a gathering in Bridges' honor hosted by these teachers. Amat drove us to the reception in her white Suzuki—her petite frame barely stretching over the steering wheel. We were carefree, happy to be cruising around the city with one of Ta'iz's first female drivers behind the wheel.

Our buoyant mood abruptly shifted gears on arrival at the door of the host's apartment. A man with a full beard, obviously a fundamentalist, solemnly opened the door. My colleague and I did not make eye contact with the host, nor did we extend our hands in greeting. We simply nodded, acknowledging gratitude for the invitation into his home.

We were directed into a salon, enthusiastically greeted by more than a dozen animated women eager to find out more about us. For nearly two hours, we answered their questions about our beliefs and values—why we volunteered with Bridges; why we travelled to Yemen; why we cherished respectful relations between faiths.

After this intense grilling, we sat on the floor to share a Yemeni meal, eating with the fingers of our right hands and talking about the program. I relaxed. Trust was palpable in the room.

After dinner, the female host, Nadia, isolated me and in Arabic commanded that I swear allegiance to Islam. I was startled, and simply pretended not to understand. The second time, I got angry, deeply angry—after talking for two hours about the value of mutual respect, how could this host now dare to demand that I claim allegiance to Islam? In my halting Arabic, body taut, I exploded.

The third time Nadia asked, the elastic band holding this tension between our faiths snapped. The pressure suddenly broke—calmly, and from the bottom of my heart, I looked into her eyes, and asked: *"Nadia, can you understand that my values and beliefs mean as much to me as yours do to you?"* And, then I hugged her, really hugged her. We stepped apart, both of us wiping away tears. This fundamentalist woman understood, accepted and respected the depth of the beliefs underlying my secular veil.

This face-to-face experience shed light, for me, on the boundaries between 'The West' and fundamentalist Islam. At first, we try to coexist at a superficial level, ignoring our differences. But, as we become more assertive in claiming the worth of our own beliefs, and rights, anger mounts and polarity becomes inevitable. When this tension breaks, recognizing each other as fellow humans is the only way we can hold the compassion and empathy required to ultimately respect our differences. Academic theorizing cannot move us past this impasse.

This fundamentalist Islamic teacher in Yemen has seen the values that lie beneath my secular veil, and I have seen the values that lie beneath her black hijab. Together, we move forward, building flesh and blood bridges to span the widening ideological chasm that threatens to divide us.

Jung compares this search for equilibrium to the quest for the Holy Grail, the sacred cup from which Jesus drank wine at the Last Supper and in which his blood was collected at his crucifixion. For many the Grail—the cup—is an ancient symbol of the female echoed in hallowed images of the female breast, mother's milk and the vulva. This cup is not a passive vessel in procreation; it is sacred. Almost a millennium has passed since the origin of the Grail legends and the need to correct masculine-feminine equilibrium has peaked once again. Like pilgrims, we burrow to the core of our *Gender Onion* alone; yet heartened to know many fellow travellers are journeying on a similar path.

It requires courage, and abundant faith, to choose to continue to engage in the struggle to hold the tensions between the secular and the spiritual. In my darkest moments, I do feel like slamming the door on all organized religion. At other times, particularly when I am weary of the struggle, I am tempted to politely smile and endure by tuning out the gender noise within my religion and placing my faith in the secular world's ability to restore equilibrium between men and women. But, it is impossible. *Wonder Woman* isn't a sufficiently satisfying icon of the sacred feminine. Unveiling misconceptions about male and female rights and roles within a faith framework remains vital to me. At this crossroad, I stand up and declare: *You have no right to make me have to choose between my feminism and my faith. My beliefs—including my belief in God and the rights of humans—mean as much to me as your beliefs mean to you.*

At times, the aim of religion can seem directly opposed to my vision of a soaring two-wingèd bird.

Nevertheless, I have to dare to lift the secular veil on my values.

Face. Artist: M. Nizar, Yemen

The Bride

I watch.

The bride's sequined white dress; her mahogany hair, bouffant-style, adorned with rhinestones, silk flowers and pastel highlights; makeup that transforms her olive complexion to pearl, heavily khol'd eyes, blood red lipstick, and rouge. I notice the intricate henna patterned on her arms and hands and feet. It takes days to prepare the henna; the bride won't have to work again until all the henna has faded.

The romance of this idea makes me ache.

This is the most sumptuous food I have ever tasted. Every delicacy is handmade by the bride's mother, sisters, sisters-in-law, cousins, aunts, grandmothers. I eat more! Look, here is Bent al-Sahn—daughter of the pan—my favorite dish lavished with honey.

Now that you've eaten, the bride's mother says to me, let me hold the incense burner to your breast, and waft its sweetness into your hair and into your dress—there—that makes you smell more exotic. More Yemeni. Don't you love the smell? Oud, frankincense and myrrh magically spun together. It will make you want to swirl, she says!

Of course, I want to dance; I want it all—the pageantry, the food, the incense, the trilling ululation! This is the moment this bride—her family and friends—have been waiting for since the day she was born.

I think of my own wedding ceremony celebrated twenty-seven years ago. Would an outsider have felt as welcomed? What would their reaction have been to seeing me, in my simple white dress, minimalist makeup and unadorned hair, walking joyfully and confidently across the expanse of lawn in front of my family's red-brick farmhouse to meet my future husband...the tassels of corn in the July field glistening with golden light to illuminate the ancient rituals and record the sacred vows:

I take thee...to have and to hold from this day forth, for better or worse, for richer or poorer, in sickness and in health, to love and to cherish, till death do us part.

Would they think: this is the moment this bride—and her family and friends—have been waiting for since this young woman was born?

This bride's face is beautiful and sensual. She has an earthy mysteriousness that is provocative. Most cultures place more value on the beauty of a woman's face than on a man's. Is it true, I wonder, that a man falls in love through his eyes and a woman falls in love through her ears?

She's young, maybe late teens, sitting perfectly still, regal in a gilded chair onstage, ready to be given away.

Young girls come up to me, giggling, and the bravest dares to touch my face and my chin-length blonde hair. She asks, her expression fretful: Why do you cut your hair...do you not have a husband?

In each of us two powers preside, one male, one female; and in the man's brain, the man predominates over the woman, and in the woman's brain, the woman predominates over the man... Coleridge perhaps meant this when he said that a great mind is androgynous. It is when this fusion takes place that the mind is fully fertilized and uses all its faculties.

Virginia Woolf, *A Room of One's Own*

Every morning I get down on my knees and thank God for not creating me a man... A man who has to take it like a man. A man who can't fake it.

Margaret Atwood, Alien Territory from *Good Bones and Simple Murders*

Chapter 6

The Individual within the Family

Weddings

Curiously, the young women at this Yemeni wedding were embarrassed for me; my sexual identity compromised by the length of my hair! In their world, I'm nearly castrated. What then, I wonder, are we to make of the ancient Israelite demand that a bride shave her head immediately upon becoming a man's wife? Shlain explains this tradition in *The Alphabet versus The Goddess*: "After shaving her scalp, a married woman must wear wigs or scarves for the rest of her life." What utterly divergent customs. Orthodox Jews demand their wives shave their heads, Muslims demand their wives cover their gorgeous hair, and Christians think nothing of shearing their hair short as fashion commands.

Castration of females isn't something we think much about. The *vagina dentata* has appeared in Picasso's art and Freud's psychology, and fear of castration "has given rise to many men's speculation that lurking just beyond the lips of a woman's vulva lies a row of sharp teeth." The woman has teeth; this does much to rationalize some men's need to control women and their reproductive organs. This also explains why Lorena Bobbitt, the battered American wife who retaliated by cutting off part of her husband's penis with a twelve-inch kitchen knife, is a cult-hero to some in the West: "If he does something like that, I'm walking away with one thing, and trust me, it's not alimony."

Certainly, there are differences between Western and Islamaic experiences with marriage; differences that cannot be seen as trifling. I took it for granted I had the autonomy to choose whom to marry. Mothers of most eligible bachelors in Yemen identify high-potential brides from trusted families, which might include blood relatives; the young man has the right of veto. In Yemen, one never underestimates the influence of a mother of sons. As the mother of *three* sons, the thought is enticing… for about a nanosecond; imagine being responsible for handpicking my sons' life partners and being accountable for their future happiness. After the marriage request is formally made by the groom's father to the bride's father, the bride-to-be technically has the independent right to say *yes* or *no* to the invitation of marriage. What courage—to look not one but two clans in the eye and decline an offer of marriage.

But, there is poignant sameness too: There is sameness in the deeply rooted *promise* of this union. Divorce happens everywhere, blemishes the symbolic significance of the ceremony. Wherever it happens, the death of mutually reciprocated love is sad—in Yemen, husbands can choose to marry a second or third or even fourth wife and divorce is technically feasible (if you consider it acceptable, or possible, for a mother to accept the potential loss of her children); in Canada, husbands and wives can agree to separate; anywhere, husbands and wives can stop loving one another. Little wonder Jesus discouraged divorce and predictably his words have shown up repeatedly in marriage ceremonies for centuries: "What God hath joined together…".

Joseph Campbell, myth expert, predicted that "when people get married because they think it's a long-time love affair, they'll be divorced very soon, because all love affairs end in disappointment…marriage is recognition of a spiritual identity."

I wholeheartedly agree.

In the West we struggle to reconcile expectations for monogamous relationships with statistics on infidelity. And, we ask: Should the wronged woman *stand by her man*? Dr Laura Schlessinger, radio show host and author of books with provocative titles like *The Proper Care and Feeding of Husbands*, blames women for their husbands' unfaithfulness. When New York's governor, Eliot Spitzer, shocked the world with his confession about employment of $1,000 an hour call girls, Dr Laura blamed his wife, Silda Wall Spitzer, Harvard-educated lawyer and wife of 20 years. "When the wife does not focus in on the needs and the feelings, sexually, personally, to make him feel like a man, to make him feel like a success, to make him feel like her hero, he's very susceptible…. The cheating was his decision to repair what is damaged and to feed himself where he is starving."

Infidelity in most relationships is choking, even more so for *the lovely wife* of a public figure. Columnist Ellen Goodman raises her eyebrow at our expectations for public wives. "We want an independent thinker who rarely contradicts her husband. We want women who are powerful but not uppity, to shine but not outshine, and above all, to be equals who happily choose to walk one step behind. We expect them to stand by their man in good times and are horrified when they do it in bad times."

Submission

The word *Islam* translates to submission. Muslim friends in Yemen are always explaining this to me. It makes me want to scream: *I understand the meaning of submission!* Born into a farming community in Canada at the end of the baby boom, I developed natural resistance that allows me to survive as a female in the sometimes inhospitable culture of patriarchy. This immunity served me well, later, working in the oil patch. In our clan, I was one of the deviants. It wasn't that obvious—I didn't have pointed ears or Medusa-like hair—but I was different. I didn't denigrate patriarchy, but I didn't submit…easily.

Both my parents were born into farming families that were inherited by sons. As the seventh child in an ambitious family of ten, with a hard-working Scotsman at the helm, my mother is fully acclimatized to clan cultures. Several of her siblings own family farms that are largely managed by nephews within multi-generational hierarchies. Applying a heavy dose of Protestant work ethic, my parents adroitly combined family-farm patriarchy with the American Dream: *equality was within reach of anyone*—including daughters—*with the courage and the will to use their God-given talents to seize the prize.*

Reality was slightly different. A family farm is more than land or a livelihood; it is a legacy passed from one generation to the next, preferably via male lineage.

You wouldn't want to have to change the name on the barn.

How different is this version of hierarchy than ancient Confucian philosophy? According to Confucius, the most important familial relationship occurred between a father and his son; the second most important was between elder and young brothers. For Confucius, ideal society—and stability—rested on obedience of wives to husbands, daughters to fathers, and mothers to sons.

Fortunately for our parents, neither my sister nor I had the temerity to ask for the farm after our younger brother arrived.

My mother, Eleanor, is an archetypal farm wife. She is a generous and hard-working woman, full of warmth and energy, and selfless to a fault. She radiates gentleness. She is a hub in the wheel of our tribe, living and breathing *Belonging* attributes. But, as my primary role model in the art of wife and motherhood, my mother wasn't able to offer me terribly appealing strategies for looking patriarchy in the eye. The relationship between my parents is one of reciprocated love and respect; but when the two tectonic plates bump into each other—my mother's *Belonging* values (mutuality, cooperation and generosity) colliding with my father's *Enterprise* values (individualism, competitiveness and materialism)—the *Belonging* values nearly always give way to the *Enterprise*.

My mother's selflessness reminds me of Margaret Atwood's revisionist version of "The Little Red Hen" story. When everyone else wants to share in the loaf of bread, women have traditionally reacted this way:

> I apologize for having the idea in the first place. I apologize for good luck. I apologize for self-denial. I apologize for being a good cook...I apologize for smiling, in my smug hen apron, with my smug hen beak. I apologize for being a hen. Have some more. Have mine.

One millstone around my hardworking parents' neck was my appetite for independence and ferocious sense of social justice. With unconditional love, my parents gave me space to reach beyond clan boundaries. "Leadership is being extended to you," my father counselled. "There is an accountability that comes with that leadership. You must learn to think beyond 'me' to 'us'."

Dad is not a student of philosophy—he is a farmer to the core—his reading list is short and practical. But, his advice has uncanny resonance with that of myth-seekers like Joseph Campbell who counsels: *When we quit thinking primarily about ourselves and our own self-preservation, we undergo a truly heroic transformation of consciousness.*

As daughter, rather than son, this thinking beyond me to us thankfully did not oblige me to stay on the farm for the sake of the name on the barn.

I married an accountant instead.

One who lived in the city, even in another province 2,000 miles away, far removed from our rural family farm. Rather curiously, I did retain my maiden name after marriage. Didn't want the name on the barn, but the family moniker did seem to have inexplicable meaning.

When my husband and I enthusiastically announced our engagement one Christmas, the clan resumed its natural defences. Who was this fiancé; what does his father do; what are his family's values? As young as thirteen, our paternal grandmother endowed my sister and me with fine china and crystal. When my younger sister married a local farmer, at the ripe age of nineteen, everyone in the neighborhood—*more than eight hundred people*—came together to celebrate the joining of these two clans. Marrying someone outside the community—and outside the reach of my tribe's circle of trust—was a serious breach of protocol.

My fate could have been far worse. If I'd been born into Confucian China instead of patriarchal North America, my mother would had been required to bind my feet to ensure that I was sexually attractive to local men. What kind of thinking could have allowed anyone to see a hobbled woman as desirable?

Gender segregation

When I was young, gender segregation was commonplace. When our clan gathered socially, the females cooked and talked about children; males smoked and talked about tobacco crops. Even before we reached puberty, my sister and I were unfazed by the expectation that we were to prepare and serve a full roast beef dinner for a dozen or so ravenous seasonal laborers harvesting corn or tobacco on our farm. Our brother would never be expected to prepare food for others.

I was passionate about softball, and played as the catcher on a girls' softball team; boys played on boys' softball teams. Now, society's *rules* on gender segregation are less precise. All my sons play hockey; until adolescence, the braver female hockey players in our community joined boys' hockey teams. In our home, gender-neutral responsibilities are continually under negotiation: Who takes out the trash, who does the gardening, who cooks dinner and cleans up, who buys groceries, who takes the boys to the doctor, who services the car?

In Yemen, gender segregation boundaries in the public domain—the classroom, the mosque and the office—are pretty well demarcated. Just like the rural community where I grew up, when Yemenis come together socially, women stay in the kitchen and talk about their children and men squat on their haunches chewing qat leaves (a shrub that produces an amphetamine-like stimulant) and talk about their work or politics.

Men seem to have a preemptive right to public spaces.

This has upside. Walking through a market, you will see men holding hands, or linking arms. Yemeni women reach out to hold my hands when we are together. At female-only qat chews or parties, I dance with other women. This simple human connection is surprisingly moving; it took me several years to become accustomed to this level of intimacy with other women. My reaction made me realize how significantly homophobia has contaminated male-to-male and female-to-female bonding in North America and many northern European countries. My sons enjoy spending time with their male buddies, but they genuinely fear being labelled *gay* by others if they demonstrate too much affection.

Pre-pubescent boys and girls are blissfully unencumbered by segregation rules in Yemen. It is an age of innocence. In the West, other than the occasional bar mitzvah, youth can slip from childhood into adolescence with little fanfare, or worse, weighed down by derisive assumptions: *teenagers have an attitude, they are rebellious.* Pubescence is fairly well understood in the West, at least anatomically; most of our knowledge is shared with schoolmates in titillating sex education classes. While not perfect, this is progress. When my grandmother had her first menses, she hid it from her family, assuming she was dying. For her, this first cycle of life-bearing blood did not carry the ancient message of wonder; rather, it bore humiliation and fear.

In the Muslim world, the transformation of child to adolescent is an acknowledged rite of passage. For Yemeni girls, the transition can be abrupt; one day you are a little girl with your hair in colored bows, the next your first menstrual bleeding starts and you must cover your blue jeans and T-shirt with a black chador, hide your hair and sometimes even your face with a veil. And, for some Yemeni girls, sexual maturity can be an abrupt launch into marriage. A 1992 Yemeni law set the minimum legal age of marriage at fifteen, but Parliament revised this law in 1998, allowing girls to be married earlier as long as they did not live with their husbands until reaching sexual maturity.

My eldest son joined me in Yemen when he was eleven. In the midst of a serious business meeting, a Yemeni colleague loudly asked if my accompanying son was *pubescent.* Taken aback by the question, I whispered: "No, Graydon isn't yet pubescent," and we resumed our work. A few days later, I understood the question: my colleague's son was being married and he wanted to know if he could invite Graydon and me to the *female* wedding ceremonies. My pre-pubescent son and I attended the wedding party; his blonde hair and blue eyes attracted a lot of attention and I will never forget his red-faced embarrassment as young Yemeni girls encircled him in dance, lithe hips provocatively mimicking the movements of their mothers and older sisters.

As a female guest in Yemeni homes, I enjoy the rare privilege of observing how Yemeni households function—without veils and chadors. One of my favorite places to be in Yemen is seated on the floor along the perimeter of a plastic tablecloth sharing a traditional lunch with a family, dipping chunks of warm flat bread into the communal clay pot of steaming *salta*, a spicy beef and potato casserole covered with green tomato foam. Listening to the family banter, it's easy to see who makes the decisions in the household and who influences those decisions. When we enter the family living room after lunch—to rest on cushions that demarcate the boundary of the room, to smoke, to talk, and to watch the muted images on the twelve-inch television in its place of honor along the otherwise unadorned feature wall—the *males* are the first to be seated, and the first to be offered tea.

This male authority is necessarily conspicuous. Men in Yemen wear jambiyas, or sheathed knives on a belt around their waists, men lead their sons to the mosque to pray, men count out the money for school fees. But, mothers influence questions about the children, their education, food purchases, faith. Fathers may offer the first opinions and the final judgments, but there can be substantial dialogue in between.

Sons and daughters

From my outsider's perspective, Yemeni parents seem to treat their sons and daughters very differently after puberty. Once boys reach adolescence, they are groomed to assume their role as head of the household; they wear jambiyas, they go to the mosque to pray. Young men become more visible in the community at precisely the same time that their adolescent sisters become invisible.

Although there is much speculation about Islam's subjugation of the girl child, what I have observed within Yemeni families is a profound preciousness; fathers' eyes and voices soften when they speak of their daughters. There seems to be a special place for daughters in a father's heart. Female infanticide is denounced as barbarous. It is considered a pre-Islamic custom of some Arabian tribes and is a criminal act within Islam. Prophet Mohammed's oft-quoted passage is recited, for my benefit: *Whoever has a daughter and he does not bury her alive, does not insult her, and does not favour his son over her, Allah will enter him into The Paradise.* Families living beyond subsistence can afford the luxury of treating their daughters like princesses.

In Yemen, birth control is not taboo, yet parents still choose to have many children. Mothers in Yemen will be pregnant, on average, a dozen times. A close family friend from Yemen, Mohammed al-Murayri, prides himself on being the youngest sibling in a family of twenty-six—his mother was the second of two wives. Imagine that family reunion.

In China, parents are told that for the sake of their country they can have only one child. Chinese parents often choose a son—even within a Communist political structure that purports to embrace equality. The one child policy was never intended to influence gender but the distortion of male to female babies is real. According to the *China Daily* newspaper—a publication sanctioned by the Chinese government—as of 2007, China has 37 million more males than females. A census in 2000 showed that the gender ratio between female and male infants was 100 to 116, widening to 100 to 119 in 2005. Regional disparities are admitted; a ratio of 100 female infants to 138 male infants is reported in southern China's Guangdong and Hainan provinces.

I wonder: would my husband and I be tempted to do the same?

In the summer of 2007, our family travelled to China. Up close, the Chinese government's edict looks stern: Chinese citizens can lose their jobs if they disobey the one child rule. Young men of marriageable age are openly competing for brides. It is predicted that 30 million Chinese men will be unable to find a bride in 2020 if these distortions continue. In a conversation with 26-year old Changwai, in a small city along the Yangtze River, this young man proudly volunteered that he was one of two siblings in his family: "I have a sister, four years older than me. My parents were allowed to have a second child, after four years, because their first child was a girl. There aren't enough girls for the males here in Yichang," Changwai laments. "It is a problem for me and my friends. We need money to get a good apartment and a good wife. It's tough to compete."

At first my sons and I were bemused by the unconcealed reverence for male offspring, especially by Chinese women: "*You are a strong mother, three sons,*" the waitress greeted me at breakfast on our first day in Xi'an.

"*These your three sons?*" asked the tour guide at the Wild Goose Pagoda. "*You very lucky*".

"*One, two, three,*" the street vendor wordlessly counted off with her fingers as our family filed past, her toothless grin widening as the testosterone tally rose.

But, the distortion became unsettling. Too much kowtowing to the masculine, even for my sons. When asked, some locals attributed this gender imbalance to a deeply rooted macho belief that boys are better than girls: "Agriculture dominated China's economy for thousands of years and there was a greater need for boys than girls in the fields;

male offspring can provide better support to the family and care for the elderly."

We struggled to align these explanations with China's Olympic swagger; this mindset seemed more closely aligned to Pearl Buck's world. The implications for Chinese families are staggering: ultrasound technology has enabled the abortion of female fetuses, and the trafficking of women and children and illegal trans-border marriages is spiraling. Looking to the future, I don't envy middle-aged Chinese couples having to care for aging parents in a one-child world. If a wife is primarily responsible for the care of her own aging parents, plus her husband's parents, how can her range of career options not be limited?

It is tempting to look at this unfolding situation in China in black and white—masculine versus feminine. It would make us feel better, somehow, if we could identify a *culprit* to blame. But, there is no single organization or individual responsible for the macho values that persevere within China's culture. In spite of Communism's endorsement of equality, women and men perpetuate discrimination: *both mothers and fathers prefer male offspring*. And, the impacts of gender distortion negatively impact males as much as females in modern day Chinese families.

At the core of the Gender Onion

Many of us are comfortable talking about sexism from the outside edges of the *Gender Onion*; to really get to the heart of issues, we need to get personal. *The little history is much more important than the big history.* In writing this book, I peppered families in China, Yemen, Canada—families everywhere—with provocative questions, much like my sons *take a poke* at their friends on Facebook. On the first poke, many were uneasy; talking about personal gender dilemmas wasn't terribly comfortable. With some gentle prodding, many let down their guard and ultimately embraced the idea of coming together on these complex questions.

In fact, breaking out of self-imposed isolation was rejuvenating. We shared stories about the sexism we experience in our own lives. We asked one another: *If you really felt like you weren't alone, what could you do?* We admitted that self-reliance and independence kept us apart; reconnecting with others was the only way forward. This invitation gave me permission to recognize, even share, my own story.

When Canada decided to embed gender equality rights in our Constitution during my tenure at law school, twenty-seven years ago, I felt invincible. Pierre Elliott Trudeau, the father of Canada's Charter of Rights and Freedoms, had presented Canadians with critical ingredients for a just society. This legal framework, combined with economic opportunity and fierce personal determination, allowed me to survive—even thrive—as a female executive within the male-dominated culture of the international energy sector.

But as a wife and mother and daughter, I quietly struggled to navigate the inner turmoil of preserving my femininity in a very masculine world. With a brave public face, I privately agonized over my choices. *In a gender-neutral society, I was rewarded for adopting masculine traits.* The worth of femininity seemed diminished, not enriched. The sweet promise of equality had gone slightly bitter. Was this really the gender legacy that I wanted to extend to future generations?

The deserts of Yemen were the last place that I expected to have my confidence in gender equality revived, a place in which Muslim women seem so obviously oppressed. Weren't deserts the place of alienation, even disenfranchisement of Biblical proportion? But I have found that patriarchy can be dreadfully obvious or insidiously subtle at this most inner layer of human interaction; like the desert, patriarchy can seem very small on the surface yet enormous underneath. Certainly, this inner layer is the most stubborn, the most resistant to change. Yet, paradoxically it is also where the most opportunity for change exists, in the West or in the East. The place where small in-roads can be made; like the desert, sometimes even the place for divine revelation.

Change happens, I believe, from the inside out, rather than the reverse. Small changes within families, incremental steps of progress for people in face-to-face interaction are vital in preparing societies for the more obvious outward changes, often the last to happen. When we understand human nature, this rings true: Big outer change happens when the time is right, when the groundwork has been laid. This is true for individuals (we can't change outwardly until we change inwardly) and it is true as well for societies. This is an empowering idea of hope.

I have found and believe that even the smallest change in interpersonal interaction is a seed planted for growth. Martin Buber said it best:

> We come alive only when we relate to others...we are here to change the world with small acts of thoughtfulness done daily rather than with one great breakthrough.

And, like Buber, I have seen flowers blooming in the desert.

The wilderness and the desert will be glad,
And the Arabah will rejoice and blossom;
Like the crocus.

Isaiah 35:1 New American Standard Bible

Chapter 7

Creating a Breathing Space

Even a positive thing casts a shadow...its unique
excellence is at the same time its tragic flaw.

~ William Irwin Thompson

Between stimulus and response there is a space.
In that space is our power to choose our response.
In our response lies our growth and our freedom.

~ Viktor E. Frankl

The humble crocus is a curious plant, poking its green shoots out of the ground in search of sunlight. These blooms are perfectly compatible with the local environment, whether it is the sand of the Middle Eastern desert or a late spring snowfall in Canada. There is beauty in their simplicity, their delicacy, and their perseverance. Most faiths see harmony in beauty; beauty offers resonance and a sense of the sacred. Buddha saw the wisdom of the whole world in the simple lotus flower. In the Middle Ages, the rose was seen as the symbol of the Virgin Mary. In Islamic culture, flowers are often seen as symbols of the Kingdom of Allah.

In *A New Earth: Awakening to your life's purpose*, author Eckhart Tolle invites us to look upon flowers as the enlightenment of plants: "*Flowers, more fleeting, more ethereal, and more delicate than the plants of which they emerged, would become like messengers from another realm, like a bridge between the world of physical forms and the formless.*" Tolle even recognizes the messengers—*Buddha, Jesus, and others, not all of them known*—as humanity's early flowers. A widespread flowering was not yet possible in their time, and their message was misunderstood and distorted, suggests Tolle. "*The world was not ready for them, and yet they were a vital and necessary part of human awakening.*"

As I went through this process, this peeling of the onion (another bulb), I realized what all flowers needed, what we all need: breathing space. This may seem like an obvious conclusion, but I asked myself what a place like this would look like, a place where everyone could breathe, a place where ideas could be exchanged in a less threatening way, a "*Geneva state of mind*". A jumping-off point from the flatness of *lowest common denominator* or *consensus-building* dialogues, two-dimensional platforms that can sometimes feel not quite uplifting enough. I asked myself if this place was even possible. And the answer is yes. Because my breathing space is far from Utopian; instead it's a place marked by imperfection, tolerance, and differences. And it's not a place of agreement, compromise, conformity or consensus. It's a place *to be*.

As much as five thousand years ago, an Indian Tantra is believed to have created this image of a breathing space: "When in worldly activity, keep attentive between the two breaths (the in breath and the out breath), and so practicing, in a few days be born anew." In *Cosmos*, Carl Sagan stepped back from Planet Earth to laud the symmetry of plants and animals each inhaling the other's exhalations.

In the Old Testament, a Psalmist spoke of a breathing space for the children of Israel that was orchestrated by Moses: "He [Yahweh] would have destroyed them, had not Moses, his chosen, stood before him in the gap to turn away his wrathful indignation."

In *Shah of Shahs*, Ryszard Kapuscinski talks about the mosque as a place to breathe: "A church is closed space, a place of prayer, meditation, and silence…. A mosque is different…. Not all those who come here are fervent Muslims, not all are drawn by a sudden wave of devotion—they come because they want to breathe, because they want to feel like people."

Psychologists speak of *liminal space* as a threshold between two different planes, a place of transition where boundaries can seem to dissolve a little. In *The King of Elfland's Daughter*, Lord Dunsany invites us to *liminal space*, asking what separates us from Elfland and other realms that lie beyond the one we inhabit? The magic of liminal space is not seeing the threshold or doorway as a barrier, but rather, as a passageway into the unknown mysterious and compelling world beyond the one we know.

Everyone has a unique perspective on what constitutes a breathing space. For me, a church is a sanctuary where stillness allows me to listen, to transcend the ordinary and open up to new dimensions. Even divine intervention. It is a respite from the madding crowds, an oasis where judgment is reserved, a breathing space for inner silence to counter the busyness of the secular world.

Space is an image we are comfortable with: we talk of *my space* and *your space*; *making space* for women at a male table; *taking space* like a warrior; *rightful space* which broaches the question of entitlement; *claiming space* was the slogan for 1960s-style feminism. We're all familiar with clutter. To create a *breathing space*, we often have to de-clutter our minds and our materialistic lives. We need a *living space*, not a *dead space*. We need to see the *space* between our thoughts; to create gaps in our stream of thinking.

You will recognize this *breathing space*. Maybe one of your children will innocently ask an astute question about traditional gender roles for fathers and mothers: *Daddy, why does Mommy have to work? Tommy's mom doesn't have to work.* Maybe one of your coworkers will scratch his or her head and ponder why female employees keep quitting in spite of your company's written policy on diversity. Maybe after listening to the evening news, one of your parents will muse about the scarcity of female political leaders and wonder aloud if males can exclusively decide what is best for your community.

Permitting breathing spaces can be daunting. In *Getting to Maybe*, authors Frances Westley, Brenda Zimmerman and Michael Patton acknowledge this fear: "We can tend to think that great social change is the province of heroes—an intimidating view of reality that keeps ordinary people on the couch." Bill Gates' wisdom to Harvard's 2007 graduating class resonates: "The barrier to change is not too little caring; it is too much complexity."

Simple is following a recipe to bake a cake. Anyone can follow the steps; and you have a measurable result—a yummy cake or a flop—in a short period of time.

Complicated is sending a rocket to the moon. You set your long-term vision; secure funding; break down the longer term objective into bite-size project steps; engage engineers and scientists; and step by sequential step achieve this momentous target.

Complex is raising a child. There is no one way to do it. Each step has multiple effects which feed back and influence the next step or decision. What is most important is asking the right questions—rather than prescribing the right answer—and establishing resilient relationships that can withstand bumps in the road.

It may be hard to believe, but it is less complex to solve the problem of sending a rocket to Mars than to provide sustained incentive to the pursuit of dynamic equilibrium between masculine and feminine.

When you encounter backlash or resistance, you may have to take what seem like tiny steps along the pathway, and gauge whether the breathing spaces will stay open long enough to allow you to bridge the polarities. To break down stalemate, I try to focus on framing questions in non-judgmental language.

When I struggled to understand how gender equality fits within the doctrines of the Lutheran faith, I asked the pastor: *I've listened to you preach on the roles and responsibilities of men and women within the Lutheran faith. I was raised as a Presbyterian—a denomination in which males and females can vote and act as faith leaders. I'm struggling to understand the more gender-restrictive Lutheran interpretation of Paul's scriptures. Can we talk?* Of course I was fuming inside, but if I saw this pastor as part of the problem, rather than part of the solution, no breathing space would have opened up.

When I was working in a large energy company, wanting to figure out how to entice more females into the International division, I appealed to the economic and legal motivators of my coworkers: *Our policy manual states that this company values diversity. That makes good business sense. The oil and gas sector traditionally employs more males than females. So, I'm not entirely sure where our company stands on gender diversity in this industry. Can we invite someone from Human Resources to talk about how to encourage diversity in our next department meeting? Maybe we could even talk about why our company values diversity…the business case?*

This isn't heroic action. But, you do need courage, tenacity and hope. Moral courage is required to choose to take that first tiny step, and later, to take quantum leaps forward across wider chasms along the pathway. Often the greatest courage is required in the decision to act in the first place, to speak truth and to be open to others speaking their truths. Sometimes we just need to stand still, to listen.

As Rebecca Solnit explains in *Hope in the Dark*, hope in the midst of tension isn't like clutching a lottery ticket on the sofa, feeling lucky; *hope is an axe you break down doors with in an emergency.* Hope isn't an insurance policy; it is a powerful surge. It is an action.

Often, the future is unknown. We must take that step forward into the thick fog without a guarantee of the outcome. Solnit invites us to reconsider how we see that darkness. She describes dark as something inscrutable, not as something terrible and says we often mistake the one for the other.

What I'm encouraging here is a visual: allowing a breathing space, a gap between two dualities (masculine and feminine, yin and yang, inhale and exhale, art and science, leadership and management, spiritual and secular, husband and wife, East and West). I'm enthralled by the vision of this space opening up—*the third dimension*—between masculine and feminine, between the sacred and the secular paths, between East and West.

At a funeral for a former neighbor—a vibrant 91-year-old man named Tom Hall—the presiding minister, the Very Revd Robert Pynn, orchestrated a breathing space for grief by giving those of us in the pews a glimpse of the ancient love that moves in an out of the spaces between.

Over a cup of tea with one of Canada's political pioneers, Flora MacDonald, this 82-year-old champion of communities in Afghanistan shares her experience with such a breathing space between faith and feminism. In 1979, Flora was appointed the first female Secretary of State for External Affairs in Canadian history; she was one of the first female foreign ministers in the world. In Afghanistan, Flora has been a longstanding advocate for girls' education, supporting clandestine schools for girls even under the Taliban. One day, as she was leaving one of these underground schools, Flora was tailed by two stern-looking men in signature Taliban turbans. This intrepid woman admitted to feeling fear, especially when one of the men came alongside and whispered: "*We know what you are doing.*" There was a tense pause. Then the man said to Flora: "*If you let my daughters go to school, we won't tell anyone.*" This breathing space could only have been created through human-to-human interface, and as Flora suggests, who knows the influence these educated daughters will have in this Taliban home.

There is no need to invent new myths or new images; they have been here all along. Confucius said: "*A true teacher is one who knows and makes known the New by revitalizing the Old.*"

Pueblo Indians celebrate the coming of age of a young girl at her first menses by setting her hair in two whorls on the sides of her head. This wearing a butterfly, explains archaeologist Kelley Hays-Gilpin in her book *Ambiguous Images*, is associated with summer, flowers, fertility, water and a utopian spiritual world. In the Bible, Jesus seems at ease with females: with his mother and Mary Magdalene, even with the adulteress who was to be stoned and the prostitute seeking forgiveness. His relationships with these women celebrate their humanity and their representation of sexuality, maternity, fertility.

The water of life—an ancient generative symbol—is right there under our feet, just below the surface of the arid desert. We just need to drill down and tap into its sweetness to relieve our parched lives. *Sometimes, we don't even know we are thirsty until someone offers us water.* Mary's name, Maria in Latin, is associated with the noun *mare*, meaning the sea. Lao-tzu uses the metaphor of horizontally flowing water to assure us: "*The great Tao flows everywhere, both to the left and to the right…it holds nothing back. It fulfills its purpose silently and makes no claims.*" Jung likened spirit to water claiming that "When spirit becomes heavy it turns to water."

The mystery of yin can be more powerful than yang; female can triumph over male with her stillness: "Water is the softest element and rock the hardest, yet waves will eventually wear rock away." And yet it is hard to separate which is supporting which, so much of the earth is liquid, even the inner core, yet the rock is essential to the whole.

So a return to images is essential. And diversity. There is diversity in breathing space—an abundance and variety. There is also aliveness and vitality.

Guided by study into the archetypal patterning of natural numbers, grounded in the wisdoms of many ancients, Dr Bernie Novokowsky explains how tensions between the *two-ness* of any duality dynamically compete and cooperate. *Masculine and feminine* are polarities that have differences and similarities; these two forces compete with each other and complement each other. Any duality—*two-ness*—has two options: The two opposites can collapse into a whole or one-ness (two become one), or the dynamic tension between the two opposites can transcend by a third force (two become three).

The first option is for duality to collapse into *one-ness*, creating the wholeness we explored with marriage: *two shall become one.* Wholeness can be appealing. But there is a catch. With wholeness, the tensions between the two opposites (masculine and feminine) fall away, and with that loss of energy, individuality and complementarity can be lost.

Two-ness can opt to allow a mutually relevant third force—a reconciling force—to hold and continuously bring together the dynamic tensions between masculine and feminine. If you are lodged between two opposing dualities—patriarchy versus equality—it may seem easier to collapse the two polarities into some inert lowest common denominator middle ground. Yet, there is no growth without this tension; the genius is in being able to hold the dualities, allowing them to energetically coexist. As Dr Novokowsky suggests, the addition of a third dimension "allows both polarities to remain whole—no denial—which is what compromise does and why compromise in favour of one over the other can never be sustainable." Carl Sagan attributes much of Sir Isaac Newton's intellectual development to his ability to hold the tension between rationalism and mysticism. It is here, in the third dimension, where the possibility for creativity and change lies.

In India, dusk and dawn are mystical times; even young children will interrupt their play to honor the time when the duality of light and dark touch one another. Perhaps they see the space in between, the *breathing space.*

Martin Buber saw the sphere between beings—the relationship between "You and I," *the realm that hides in our midst, in the between*—as the source of meaning and revelation.

Sometimes it is easier to recognize a breathing space from this third dimension. It was Sagan who encouraged us to imagine ourselves as visitors *"from some other and quite alien planet, approaching Earth with no preconceptions."* From this viewpoint, what could masculine-feminine harmonization look like?

When you are in the middle of a bridge, suspended between the two piers firmly lodged on either bank of a river, you aren't on either side. *You are in a breathing space.*

While the breathing space is a neutral zone—that Geneva kind of place where seeds of change are sown, a creative space where new ideas are allowed to be explored, the *third hand*—there is also a breathing space within each one of us. A place we find ourselves, let ourselves off the hook, restore our sense of spirituality, gender, wholeness.

Tolle encourages us to see the space between ourselves and the roles that we are playing. When you play roles, Tolle suggests—the macho male, the middle class housewife, the victim, the protective mother, the witch—you are usually not even aware that you are playing a role. When you catch yourself doing it, that recognition creates a space between you and the role and is the beginning of freedom from that role. To avoid getting trapped in our own story—the script that we create for ourselves based on a role—Tolle encourages us to step out of the voice in our head, the thought processes, and their reflection in our body as emotion. In that inner spaciousness, that stillness, we can find our true self. We need space—*space to be, to really see ourselves and one another.*

Prophet Mohammed assures us: *"The faithful are mirrors to one another."* Imagine the potential for peace if the faithful in the Muslim world and in the West can hold up mirrors to one another to really see what lies behind the masks preventing men—and women—from recognizing the sacred feminine.

Former President of Iran, Mohammed Khatami recommends immersion into another culture as a way to see *ourselves:*

We could know ourselves by taking a step away from ourselves and embarking on a journey away from self and homeland and eventually attaining a more profound appreciation of our *true identity*. It is only through immersion into another existential dimension that we could attain mediated and acquired knowledge of ourselves in addition to the immediate and direct knowledge of ourselves that we commonly possess. Through seeing others we attain a hitherto impossible knowledge of ourselves.

When I journey to other cultures, away from *self and homeland*, it is relatively easy to hold open breathing spaces with like-minded people like my friend Dr Ahlam binBriek in Yemen—people campaigning to reduce maternal mortality rates, female genital cutting and the stoning of young girls. Not surprisingly, it is more of a challenge to permit a breathing space with those seeking to perpetuate the status quo in places like Yemen.

Ironically though, it can sometimes be even more challenging to allow a breathing space closer to home, within my own culture and even amidst friends and family. When I see my Western friends' faith in the unilateral ability of military defence systems to assure a safe home for our families—and their diminished trust in constructive engagement as strategy critical to the building of global peace—I'm tempted to hold my breath. I have to keep reminding myself: Dynamic tension between different worldviews, open and closed, can be positive and constructive. I must be able to hold even tense dialogues open; to listen to others who have a different worldview and do everything possible to help us, together, to unearth our common humanity.

Collapsing into victimhood—as a response to a deep sense of injustice between East and West, haves and have-nots, feminine and masculine— is tempting. Yet, victimhood can be blinding and immobilizing. Farid Esack, South African Muslim activist, warns us of the risks of hovering in our own cocoons seeing only our own hurts and our own pains: *we become oblivious to the humanity that is reflected in others, and it is ultimately not in our own reality that we find the presence of God, but in others.*

Breathing spaces—between men and women, between East and West, and within the West and within the Muslim world—need to be stretched, opened wider.

It's not necessary to agree; it's necessary to keep talking.

And so I must tell you I have a secret. I've really already imparted it to you: The best way to see these great green shoots, these flowers growing, the best way to negotiate this breathing space, is from the ground. You can't see them from an airplane, or from a high tower; you have to stand on the flat ground. In many fairy tales, the chivalrous king of the land climbs into a high tower or castle. Moses did the same on a mountain. From this lofty place, the leader looks down on his people and undertakes to look after them, to heal them. Yet, even with benevolence, such heights create distortions. How is it possible for hierarchical leaders to see individuals, much less flowers poking their heads through the desert floor? Breathing space can't be legislated from the top.

Is it possible from such heights to hold the "*I and Thou*" attitude towards the world that Martin Buber encourages, or is a more detached "*I and It*" relationship inevitable? On the ground, face-to-face, it is much easier for human beings to be aware of one another with mutuality and reciprocity, as fellow subjects, rather than as subject-to-object. Such "I and Thou" human engagement allows us to hold our own ground and be open to others; to hold our space without shutting others out. It is the *relationship* between "I and Thou" that enables us to bridge the gaps between the public world and our private feelings.

For me, the rallying symbol that this vertigo is ending, that this debilitating imbalance is drawing to a close, is the great green shoots of flowers poking their heads through the desert floor. With that single grounding image, I am convinced of the potential for dynamic equilibrium between male and female. Together, East and West can restore a more natural equilibrium by celebrating the uniqueness of feminine and masculine, and recognizing the value of both in men and in women. We can cease to measure human success solely on the basis of rational intellect, logos, and achievements glorified within the public spheres of life.

This internal struggle to pare down the onion, to pare away all the layers, is important. Each layer of the *Gender Onion* plays a part in who we are as individuals, and all are necessary. Each layer becomes more personal as we go deeper inside, yet we get closer to the universal truth of equilibrium between masculine and feminine, if one exists. The deeper we journey, the more we realize how much we have in common.

Isn't each breath—*an inhale and an exhale*—the essence of the thing we have in common with every other living creature? Inside that breathing space, between those highly contentious and overly debated "*ribs*" lie the lungs that fill with air and hope, the need for that air unique to every creature on earth. And between those lungs?

A beating heart.

The future has an ancient heart.
~ Carlo Levi

People fall again and again into the same hole; they will seem to have gained a little ground, but they fall in again. This goes on repeatedly—but there is always a little bit of the hole filled in, a few of the gains retained. When they next fall into the trap, there is the feeling, "Oh! I've been here before, and I managed to get out."

Marie-Louise von Franz, *Animus and Anima in Fairy Tales*

Woman's greatest achievement, it is declared, is to be the mother of a great man.

Susan Griffin, *Woman and Nature: The roaring inside her*

Chapter 8

Raising Sons

A riddle: what do you get when you combine one open-minded yet traditionally raised man, one pioneering woman, and three sons?

Our home at times feels like a life-sized Petri dish, an alchemical experiment to see how long we can sustain dynamic equilibrium between masculine and feminine. When does life just explode in a hormone-laced volcano, or implode into weary inertness? There are times the teeter-tottering of masculine and feminine balance in our home gets woefully out of whack, when it seems my men perceive me with horror. Sensing the horror, I am gripped by an absurdly escalating rise of panic, a mix of abject fear and desperate humor: Is there hope for us on this seemingly misaligned planet or even within my own home? I smile inwardly, and the words of Marbod, eleventh-century bishop of Rennes, come to mind: "*Of the numberless images that the crafty enemy [the devil] spreads for us...the worst...is woman, bad stem, evil root, vicious fount...honey and poison.*"

It's not that bad, surely!

Much of the time there is warmth, nurturing and growth.

In the process of writing this book, as I peeled away the layers of my own onion—in ways I truly couldn't have comprehended until this undertaking—there were extraordinary transformations that happened within me. I looked at parts of my own life differently: my worldview, my outward purpose, my spirituality, my interpersonal relationships. Ultimately, everything I thought about myself and who I was became clearer in the process. I caught fleeting glimpses of the "little kernel of gold" that Thomas Merton spoke of—my essence—that core from which my aliveness, and freedom to be who I am, originates. I realized that in order for things to change in the world, change has to start at the most fundamental of levels, at the very inner layers of this onion. And one of the most pressing questions for me became: how precisely could I be interacting in interpersonal male-female relationships of my own, and perhaps most importantly of all, *how am I raising my sons?*

In the *I Ching*, the Book of Changes, the woman of the house is responsible for the well-being of the family; the mother is the binding force—the cement—that brings everyone together. Shlain describes this binding force as dough: "Yeast is a metaphor for things of the earth that rise and grow: children maturing, grain stalks shooting up, the tumescence that signifies male sexual desire—all rise. Growth is implicitly associated with the female. Dough, composed of four elemental feminine symbols— water, salt, grain, and yeast—becomes the quintessential foodstuff called 'the staff of life'."

Early in our marriage, my husband was empathetic to my high hopes for gender equality as a right enshrined in the Canadian Charter of Rights and Freedoms, financially supporting my choice to take a low-paying summer research job to flesh out gender rights under the Charter while I was in law school. As I moved into the world of work more permanently, we shared parenting and family responsibilities. We've lived, assiduously, by the rule that one of us had to be in Calgary at all times; a simple rule that has served our family well. My husband's dynamic fathering has provided a balancing role model. Yet I'm wary of this notion of parenting roles, for either my husband or me. It is easy to let being a parent swamp your whole identity, to overemphasize and even exaggerate that one aspect of your being and, without awareness, compromise yourself and your children.

Parenting aside, we had both missed the point in a way: We saw gender equality as a women's movement dependent on male support and encouragement. My husband thought he was helping liberate me to make choices. Yet, it isn't enough for my husband, and now my sons, to stand along the sidelines and root for me. They need to get into the game as participants.

Which brings me back to parenting. What does it take to raise sons who participate in gender equality, while retaining a fully balanced sense of their own masculinity?

All three of my sons are strong in math and science, love the competition of sports, and are comfortable taking physical risks. Our eldest son was the first male Glans to arrive in his generation. There was no barn to put a name on, but there was a generational reaction to his birth; an affirming sense of continuity verging on immortality. I wonder if the reaction would have been the same if they were daughters.

Of course, I'm grateful. These are fine young men. Yet, I can't help wondering; did my husband and I do something to subdue their femininity, or to over-emphasize their masculinity? Wasn't it Roosevelt who believed in rough, manly sports to prepare men for war...pent-up aggression needs some release before it becomes toxic? Maybe we do this to males all the time. We expect men to work in the most dangerous and dirty jobs. Perhaps, without my knowing, my sons have integrated all of society's subtle messages.

There is no denying that boys and girls have biological differences that cannot be ignored. Getting a handle on the *biology is destiny* argument is critical to raising sons, or daughters. The usual starting point in this discussion (after Adam and Eve) is to dissect the roles of males and females during hunter/gatherer times in history. During these stages in human development, physical attributes influenced the spheres and primary roles assumed by males and females. But contributions were non-hierarchical and equally critical to survival of the species. There was balance. Male and female archetypes have their origin in these times: The feminine archetype is the nurturer, the giver and sustainer of life, the one who seeks to keep families together; the masculine archetype is the protector, the aggressive competitor who saves the family from harm.

Humankind evolved. We made the transition to agricultural communities, experienced the industrial revolution and now globalization of our economic and communication systems. Evolution shook up sex-based archetypes, and upset the balance.

These sex-based distinctions are the obvious ones talked about in the raising of children of different genders. But, I suspect there is something much more intimate, much more subtle going on here. My sons look to me, their mother, for nurturing, for sympathy when they are wounded or hurt. And, truth be told, I like to mother them especially when they are suffering. It is heartwarming to cook their favorite meal when they are discouraged, to listen when they need consoling, simply to hold them. I don't have daughters, but if I did, wouldn't I mother them the same, with unconditional love?

Why does a mother's devotion to a son have the potential to be more monstrous than devotion to a daughter?

I suspect something different happens between mothers and sons. Even though some of this seems destined to remain an inscrutable mystery, I try to fit the puzzle pieces together.

Michael Gurian, author of *Mothers, Sons, and Lovers*, issues a stern warning:

> ...the great tension for a mother raising children, especially sons, is to balance her respect for the son as an individual with her awesome power to consume

and devour the son's fragile masculinity in her femininity. *He goes on, ...a mother will sacrifice for her son and ask in exchange that her son provide for her, protect her, be there for her, bring gifts back to her, and never leave her—but can she sacrifice so much that she asks too much in return, so that her son is never able to find out what gifts are his, not hers, what world is his, not hers?*

Jung and others predict as necessary to healthy male development the need for man to reject his mother. *Why don't daughters have to reject their mothers in the same way?* This distracting notion jars me from time to time and especially when my sons challenge my judgment. I can hear the cosmic slash of the scissors severing the apron strings; it echoes the razor-sharp slicing of the knife through their umbilical cord the day they were born.

Anthropologist, Sherry Ortner echoes this theory, "every boy loves the first woman in his life his mother. However, in order to become a man, he must reject her values so that he can be free to identify with many ones. A girl does not experience this ambivalence; she can love and continue to identify with her mother since she aspires to emulate her." This inescapable male dilemma has led to the devaluation of women in every society Ortner studied.

Perhaps there is even an innate patronizing quality within the collective feminine that is in need of change before we can eradicate patriarchy? I asked myself if perhaps this has been our "collective revenge," our answer to physical dominance and hierarchies, a patronizing of our sons which keeps them from their true potential, denying them an inner strength that ultimately might require their rejection of us...all out of our own need to be needed?

This is all so utterly complex.

As a mother of sons, I care that males seem to have inherited crippling body-pain. That cumulative feeling of defeat—that discouragement and disappointment—is a burden that men seem prone to carrying around with them. It is unsettling to me, unnatural, that many of the adult men seeking the counsel of my Canadian colleague, Dr Jagdeep Johal, speak of this deeply embedded feeling that can be overwhelmingly out of proportion to the reality of a present-day situation. Even before men embark on a new and exciting project, Dr Johal finds them weary, already plodding in hip waders through the muck of disappointment. Male DNA seems to be encoded with a universal message: "Don't get too excited, your expectations won't be met". Or maybe the message is "Don't get too excited. You are what you do and if you fail at what you do, you are nothing."

I can understand women connecting to collective martyrdom—that feeling that activates just before menstruation. But, where do males plug into this universal disappointment and why does it seem more insidious than females' body-pain? Maybe males have inherited more blame. What a paradox: do sons need to reject their mothers to mask their cosmic guilt for the role they play, as males, in suppressing the worth of the feminine?

This feeling of disappointment can be overwhelming for males, and dangerously addictive. In the Middle East, the weight of this collective disappointment in males—this negativity—can be nearly unbearable.

As a mother, I try to teach my sons to shake off any insidious rush of discouragement; to rid themselves of these toxic thoughts like a dog flings water from its fur. I encourage them to be rationally exuberant about their future. I coach them to be on the lookout for signs of masculine-feminine imbalance, and they are getting better and better at recognizing and navigating gender dilemmas. They are fully alert, aware of the risk of being manipulated and co-opted as Caucasian males.

Having sons is the most meaningful thing I've ever done; it is the most intensely joyous experience that my husband and I have shared. Birthing was a mystical event: I carry the cycle of life within.... It pulses through my veins: motherhood, daughter, motherhood. I'm the Queen Bee, carrying ideas from one generation to the next, like a honeybee carries pollen; even carrying ideas from West to East and back again.

Being female, biologically, I now honor and emulate the very Goddess values that our modern society has tried to conceal: sexuality, fertility, maternity. For years, I was guarded about how and when I spoke of motherhood. A woman in a man's world, I went deep inside and found meaning in the inner layers of my *Gender Onion* yet struggled to reconcile these core values with my role as a professional woman of the world. How many years have I slumbered, subconsciously condoning devaluation of the feminine?

Women aren't going to single-handedly save the world, and neither are men. We don't live in a male world and we don't live in a female world; we all need awakening. Men need to be given the chance to let themselves off the hook. They need to breathe, deeply, and fill up the spaces between the layers of their *Gender Onion*, and lift their hearts. They need to know, for themselves, what a rainbow of choices can look like—this notion of gender equilibrium isn't about creating icons that only females can grasp.

I'm curious to see how my sons raise their children. I have such big expectations.

The atmosphere is honey-sweet in our home. Our garden is chock-full of alliums, hardy perennials that survive the cold winters in Calgary and explode out of their bulbs through the snow into spiky purple blooms. The "White Sahara," that's what singer Susan Aglukark calls the Canadian North. I smile at the memory of my youngest son's childhood affection for the alliums' bloom. He would race around the yard holding bouquets in one hand high above his head, making the pop-pop and swishing sound of explosions. For him, these fireworks flowers were charged, loaded.

As I am writing, jolting news from Yemen disrupts my sanctuary: Al-Qaeda has just claimed credit for a bomb attack on an apartment block where foreigners reside in Yemen's capital city of Sana'a. This attack follows on the heels of the cold-blooded murders of two Yemeni males, drivers in a tourist caravan traversing the Hadhramout desert and two tourists from Belgium, both female. These murders took place in Wadi Do'an, a valley in the Hadhramout I know well. Horrific murders like this are intended to drive stakes between the Muslim world and West.

Other murders come to mind.

In 2006, I was invited to Afghanistan to serve the interests of women emerging from Taliban rule. My reaction to this invitation was a primal showdown between hope and fear, open versus closed. Hope prevailed. Within days of acceptance of this invitation, my optimism was crushed by the Taliban's cold-blooded murder of a critical local partner in this work. Safia Ama Jan—Women's Affairs director in Kandahar and longstanding champion of female education in Afghanistan—was gunned down in front of her home on September 25, 2006. I cancelled my flight to Afghanistan.

Five months later, in Punjab province, Pakistan, an Islamist gunman assassinated Zil-e-Huma Usman, women's rights activist and Minister for Social Welfare. She was shot dead by a bearded lone attacker while meeting with party workers at her political office on February 20, 2007. The murderer—Mohammad Sarwar—was suspected in the killing of other women, but has not been charged for lack of evidence. According to local police, Sarwar believed it was contrary to the teachings of God for a woman to become a minister or a political ruler.

At the close of 2007, the world reeled with the murder of Pakistan's opposition leader Benazir Bhutto.

All three women held official government positions. Safia had served as chief of the Woman's Affairs department in Kandahar for five years; Zil-e-Huma had just been appointed to a ministerial position. Benazir's political pedigree is well known. That these women were more compelling targets to Islamic militants because of their public leadership roles is telling. Although we will never know with certainty, it is probable that each of these women knew fear. There must have been days when each woman would have preferred anonymity; would have preferred a closed worldview. And, surely their families knew fear. Safia was the mother of a teenaged son and wife to a husband disabled by paralysis; Zil-e-Huma was a wife, and mother of two sons. The world is well acquainted with Benazir's family.

Many have already forgotten Safia in Kandahar, and Zil-e-Huma in Punjab. In their wake, thousands of men and women in Afghanistan and Pakistan—and in the rest of the Muslim world—resolutely continue their march, advocating for women's rights and modeling courage for their children and grandchildren. Every day, these individuals choose hope over fear. For those of us with an open worldview—who see the interconnectedness of humanity and equality—the survival of this worldview is critical, in the Muslim world and in the West. Yet, it is not easy to hold the tension. Sometimes it is tempting to just quietly close the door.

Now, my three sons edge closer and closer to the perimeter of our family nest. One day they will be sufficiently independent to soar away to their own heights. Their evolution from infant to child to adolescent to adult has been a joy to observe. Right now, they are observing me; I can feel their questions boring straight through my resolve. They want to know how I'm going to react to the recent Al-Qaeda murders in Yemen. A stern tone of voice masked over his gentle nature, the eldest wonders aloud if security is to be trusted in Yemen: "Mom, how can you keep travelling to Yemen if they can't protect you from Al -Qaeda?" His younger brothers don't verbalize their apprehension but creased brows and crossed arms tell me as much.

My sons are much taller and stronger than I am now. Being enveloped in their chivalry is tempting. Yet I'm wary of succumbing entirely within this protective embrace. They understand how passionate I am about this work— and all three have been alongside me working in Yemen. They see how their father trusts my judgment; he doesn't expect me to kowtow subserviently to his unilateral opinion. Yes, I decide, I'm getting a bit nervous of their protective, masculine tone. The last thing I want is for my sons to see me, their mother, as some frail, fragile birthing vessel they must protect.

I look at my sons and they smile tentatively. For a single moment, the world within our look is not a shared one. What is needed to choreograph this age-old dance, to allow my sons and I, as poet John Donne inspires, to possess one world?

Maybe I need to stop focusing on the two-dimensional—the dance between male and female polarities—and instead, pay attention to the third dimension.

What will it take to harmonize the masculine-feminine dynamic, to retain the good in ancient traditions, and yet move toward the enlightened…to free up the aerodynamics needed to give flight to this two-wingèd bird? Perhaps nothing more than a little wind, a bit of breathing space.

My *face in thine eye, thine in mine appears,*
And true plain hearts do in the faces rest;
Where can we find two better hemispheres
Without sharp north, without declining west?

John Donne, The Good-Morrow

Epilogue

That bird lifts his wing, one tip touches East, one West.

~ Rumi

I think back. I can see myself that day sitting across from my dear friend, Dr Ahlam binBriek, at that restaurant table in Mulkulla alongside the Arabian Sea. Together, Ahlam and I have held the tension, aware in our hearts and souls of what needs to change, yet respectful of the lines we can't yet cross. The lines reflected in the frowns and furrowed brows we see on each other's faces.

When I invited Ahlam to read this book's manuscript, this fully veiled Muslim woman wept: "You hold a mirror to me, and see me, fully."

And then I realized: Mother, professional, friend from the deserts of Yemen—Ahlam has held—and holds—a mirror up to my own life. This exotic, foreign woman from the East has, over the years, helped me put the pieces of my own kaleidoscope into some kind of recognizable order.

When Ahlam first read about herself and her son, Ali, in "Poison in the Honey", she asked if I would change her name to "Fatima" to protect her family. I wholeheartedly agreed. Then I received this message:

Dear Donna
Assalaam Alukim

Regarding my name in your book, never mind, i think you write my name as Ahlam, since i told you write other name i was not comfortable i did not did bad things.

Much love
Ahlam

It was my turn to weep.
We are making this journey together.

Gratitude

Writing a book to peel away sensitive layers of the *Gender Onion* and to unveil gender equality aspirations—in the Muslim world and in the West—can be seen by some as utter folly. In the absence of hope, such a book would have been cruel. Deeply embedded polarization of masculine and feminine casts dark shadows that can't be easily whitewashed. And, this book doesn't set out to *pink wash* or over-simplify the complexity of gender equality dilemmas. Instead, this book has its origin in an intuitive place deep within me, and is written to honestly evaluate not only where we are on gender equality, but also, to look ahead to where we are capable of going.

Without the support of others, I would never have been able to sustain the will to speak these truths. There were times when I lost faith in this project. Would anyone listen to the messages? Well-funded interest groups are dedicated to sustaining the divides between gender, and between Islam and the West. The rhetoric is daunting, intimidating even; was there any possibility for constructive changes in our reality? Logic screamed caution, discretion, even fear.

Yet, without fail, whenever I faltered, someone would appear to pick me up and set me back on my path. Sometimes it was a call from a friend organizing a gathering of women to talk about reconciling motherhood and work; sometimes it was a raw story shared by a male colleague exposing deep wounds and self-doubt; sometimes it was a "*normal*" family in our community struggling, behind closed doors, to deal with eating disorders or abuse. It was a male cousin in Detroit, John Darnbrook, who saw the worth of my stories about personal relationships with Yemeni men and women, ultimately introducing me to Lynn Fay, a dedicated editor and indefatigable champion of honest writing. Lynn's commitment to this project was vital.

And, always, there were people in Yemen who held up a mirror to my way of thinking, allowing me to see my values more clearly. People like Jamila al-Raiby, Ahlam binBriek, Emam Al-Kobati, Afrah Thabet, Mohammed al-Murayri, Osama al-Eryiani, Nagiba al-Madhi, Adel Bahameed.

To name but a few of those in the West who made this writing possible, let me express gratitude to those men and women who invigorated me, trusted me, nurtured me, even reading chapters of the manuscript: Molly Naber-Sykes, Ronnalee McMahon, Barbara Thrasher, Patricia Klinck, Shelly Barnec, Patricia Gilmore, Janis Wall, Stephanie Garrett, Frances Wright, Donna and Skye Friesen, Bernie Novokowsky, Sheri-D Wilson, Lynne Rach, Allan Pedden, Janice Eisenhauer, Annabelle Moore.

Allow me also to specially mention three male colleagues who were consulted, frequently, for male perspective and wisdom: Dr Jagdeep Johal and Revd Clint Mooney, both Canadians, and Yemen's Dr Al-Karim Eryiani.

The art of Lynnie Wonfor, the photography of Patrick McCloskey, and the creative images of Paul Smith, Bridges Webmaster, breathed life into this expedition into the heart of choice and Islam.

The professional and guiding hand of my editor at Pari Publishing, Maureen Doolan, is reflected in every page of this book. And, the wisdom shared by David Peat of the Pari Center for New Learning was profoundly synchronistic. The commitment to this book's successful unveiling demonstrated by Pari Publishing's Managing Director, Eleanor Peat, and Designer, Andrea Barbieri, was exceptional.

To my husband, Laurie, and sons, Graydon, Mitchell and Liam, your willingness to see gender equality as an aspiration that involves males and females—your willingness to not just stand alone the sidelines and cheer me on, but to *get into the game as participants*—is the foundation I needed to write this book, and more importantly, to live our life together with compassion and wisdom.

To each one of you, I'm grateful. No woman is an island.

Sources

Prologue

▷ Karl Paul Reinhold Niebuhr (1892-1971) was a Protestant theologian famous for his opinions on the danger of elevating American democracy by vilifying communism. A reissue of a collection of Niebuhr's lectures, *The Irony of American History* (University of Chicago Press, 2008), originally published in 1952, provided critical source material for this book, including quotes included in Chapter 2. The enduring relevance of Niebuhr's philosophy was affirmed in the 2008 US election campaign: "[Niebuhr] is one of my favorite philosophers. I take away [from his works] the compelling idea that there's serious evil in the world, and hardship and pain. And we should be humble and modest in our belief we can eliminate those things. But we shouldn't use that as an excuse for cynicism and inaction. I take away…the sense we have to make these efforts knowing they are hard."—Senator Barack Obama.

▷ You can learn much about Yemen's rich history by reading the biographies of early Western explorers in these regions. One of the most famous female visitors to Mulkulla was Freya Stark, a British traveler. In *The Southern Gates of Arabia: A journey in the Hadhramout*, Ms. Stark's stories are introduced by Jane Fletcher Geniesse (Modern Library, 2001). *The Passionate Nomad: The life of Freya Stark* (Modern Library, 2001) is also recommended. For further insight into the experiences of Western female pioneers in the Maghreb, Georgina Howell's biography of Gertrude Bell is also illustrative: *Daughter of the Desert: The remarkable life of Gertrude Bell* (Pan Macmillan, 2007). For more contemporary stories of life in Yemen, *Tears of Sheba* by Yemeni female, Khadija Al-Salami, published by John Wiley & Sons in 2003, is recommended.

▷ Before embarking on my first visit to Yemen, I turned to the expertise of locals and read as much as was written on Yemen by Western experts. The research of British historian, Paul Dresch, author of *A History of Modern Yemen* (Cambridge University Press, 2000) and *Tribes, Government, and History in Yemen* (Clarendon Paperbacks, Oxford, 1993) significantly enriched my understanding of Yemeni culture and history.

Chapter 1: Introduction

▷ The introductory chapter of this book begins with a quote by Osho, Indian philosopher. For more on Osho, *The Book of Wisdom: Discourses on Atisha's seven points of mind training* by Osho, Bhagwan Shree Rajneesh (Osho International, 2001) is recommended.

▷ Jungian theory on animus and anima can be accessed directly through the writings of C.G. Jung, but for perspectives on gender, I particularly appreciate the insights of Jung's student, Marie-Louise von Franz, including her following works: *Animus and Anima in Fairy Tales* (Inner City Books, 2002); *The Golden Ass of Apuleius* (Shambhala, 1992); and *Lectures on Jung's Typology,* by von Franz and James Hillman (Spring Publications, 1986).

▷ Sufi wisdom and the theories of Taoist and other Eastern beliefs were accessed directly from adherents of these faiths, including spiritual leaders. I also carried with me, in Yemen, a copy of *The Garden of Truth: The vision and promise of Sufism, Islam's mystical tradition* by Seyyed Hossein Nasr (HarperOne, 2007) and find much inspiration in *The Rumi Collection* edited by Kabir Helminski (Shambhala Classics, 2000).

▷ Discussions with Dr Jagdeep Johal of Calgary, Canada were helpful in understanding his depth of experience with men and gender. Dr Johal also shared a copy of a slim booklet, *The Human Male: A men's liberation draft policy* by Harvey Jackins and others, Rational Island, 1999 that proved quite useful.

▷ Theories on God and empire are fashionable at present: I appreciated being directed to *God and Empire* by John Dominic Crossan (HarperOne, 2007).

▷ Late night discussions in Yemen with fellow Bridges' volunteer Patricia Gilmore, introduced me to the theories of *my way, the way, a way, our way.* These ways of thinking are shared in *Paths of Change* by Will McWhinney (Sage Publications, rev. edn., 1997) and *Creating Paths of Change* by Will McWhinney, James Webber, Douglas Smith and Bernie Novokowsky (Sage Publication, 2nd edn., 1997).

▷ Envisioning gender identity as a kaleidoscope was triggered by the cover of Helen Luke's book, *Kaleidoscope: The way of women and other essays* (Parabola Books, 1992). Inspiration for this writing was derived from the writing of Carol Lee Flinders; two of her books are particularly recommended: *At the Root of this Longing: Reconciling a spiritual hunger and a feminist thirst* (Harper, 1998) and *Rebalancing the World: Why women belong and men compete and how to restore the ancient equilibrium* (Harper, 2002).

Chapter 2: The Individual in a Globalizing World

▷ Chapter 2 is introduced with two quotes: an observation on dialogue by Maurice Friedman, author of *Martin Buber: The life of dialogue* (University of Chicago Press, 1955), and an Aboriginal image of worldview shared by Hyemeyohsts Storm in *Seven Arrows* (Ballantine Books, 1973).

▷ Tony Blair's perspectives on open and closed worldviews were derived from his October 26, 2007 speech to an academic and corporate audience in Calgary, Canada.

▷ Much insight on the value of diversity was found in a reading of James Surowiecki's book, *The Wisdom of Crowds* (Anchor Books, 2005); quotes are drawn from Part 1 of Surowiecki's book.

▷ The research referenced to correlate gender diversity and country stability includes Carleton University's "Country Indicators for Foreign Policy Project", details are accessible on the university's website. For opinions on the links between gender diversity and country stability in Afghanistan, the opinions of Cheryl Benard, Senior Political Scientist with RAND Corporation and Director of the RAND Initiative for Middle Eastern Youth were useful. Benard's work includes a contribution to Volume 32, Winter 2008 edition of the *Fletcher Forum of World Affairs* entitled: "Caution Nation-Builders: Gender Assumptions Ahead".

▷ Lesley Hazleton's theories on the Jezebel treatment of women in politics are explored in her book, *Jezebel: The untold story of the Bible's harlot queen* (Doubleday, 2007) and in Hazleton's many contributions to *Time* magazine and the *New York Times*.

▷ Gloria Steinem's quotes were derived from her op-ed published in the January 8, 2008 edition of the *New York Times* titled, "Women Are Never Front-Runners". Margaret Thatcher's quotes were extracted from *The Collected Speeches of Margaret Thatcher* by Margaret Thatcher (HarperCollins, 1st edn., 1998).

▷ Canadian experience with gender equality in politics is reviewed in *The Persons' Case: The origins and legacy of the fight for legal personhood* by Robert J. Sharpe and Patricia I. McMahon (The Osgoode Society for Canadian Legal History, University of Toronto Press, 2007). Efforts of the Famous 5 Foundation, founded by Frances Wright, also keep the history and ongoing worth of female political participation alive for Canadians. Anne McLellan's perspectives on females in politics were derived from both private discussions and public addresses, including Ms McLellan's February 7, 2008 lunch address to attendees of the Women's Executive Network Top 100 Forum.

▷ The interview with Sylvia Ssinabulya, Member of Parliament in Uganda, took place in my home in June 2008, and was organized by Dr Jean Chamberlain of Save the Mothers Foundation.

▷ On the topic of globalization, several of Thomas Friedman's books were helpful sources. Quotes included in Chapter 2 are excerpted from *The Lexus and the Olive Tree* (Anchor Books, 2000).

▷ Under the heading "Reconciling universality and indigenous values", references to Mel Gray's research are derived from an article published in the *International Journal of Social Welfare* 2005: Volume 14, entitled "Dilemmas of international social work: paradoxical processes in indigenization, universalism and imperialism" (Blackwell Publishing, 2005). Phil Fontaine's quotes are derived from his op-ed published in the *Canadian National Post* on January 25, 2008. Arthur Solomon's prayer is from his book, *Songs for the People: Teachings on the natural way* (NC Press, 1990); I was first introduced to Solomon's prayer in Bill Phipps' book, *Cause for Hope: Humanity at the crossroads* (Wood Lake Publishing, 2007).

▷ The 2006 international women's conference referenced under the subheading *Discerning intention* was the second Women as Global Leaders Conference, organized by Zayed University and hosted March 12-14, 2006 in Abu Dhabi, under the patronage of HH Sheikha Fatima Bint Mubarak, President of the UAE Women's Union. I was an invited speaker; the conference attracted more than 1200 delegates from 87 countries.

▷ Benazir Bhutto's opinions and quotes were verified in her book, *Reconciliation: Islam, democracy, and the West,* posthumously published by HarperCollins in 2008.

▷ Under the heading *Unpacking Terrorism,* Niebuhr sources are as described in this book's Prologue. Peter Robb's book, *Midnight in Sicily* (Vintage, 1999), inspired thinking on the space between government and communities. The 2007 Commonwealth Report, *Civil Paths to Peace,* was written by the Commonwealth Commission on Respect and Understanding, and is recommended as an excellent source for exploration of peace-building. I was first introduced to this report in a November 10, 2007 edition of *The Economist.* Alan Greenspan's quote is from his 2007 memoir, *The Age of Turbulence: Adventures in a new world* (Penguin Press, 2007). The strategy of Hazel Blears, Communities Secretary in Britain, including the Whitehall source, were sourced from an article in the *Sunday Times,* January 6, 2008, entitled "Muslim women to curb terror" written by Marie Woolf, Whitehall editor. The Prelude to Helen Luke's *Kaleidoscope* (Parabola Books, 1992), and titled "The Bridge to Humility", is the source of the powerful idea of humility as the means to release humanity from the tension between hubris and inertia.

▷ In the final section of this chapter, the quote from Lamya al-Sakkaf was extracted from an email sent to me in 2007 in response to solicitations for Yemeni opinions on gender equality within the Muslim faith. The referenced *Foreign Affairs* article quoting Ambassador Swanee Hunt is in the May/June 2007 edition, published by the Council on Foreign Affairs; the article is titled, "Let Women Rule". I was introduced to Dr Sima Samar at an event hosted in Calgary by Women4Women in Afghanistan, on January 31, 2008 at the University of Calgary.

Chapter 3: The Individual in the Workplace

▷ The introductory quotes are excerpted from Marie-Louise von Franz's book, *Animus and Anima in Fairytales* (Inner City Books, 2002) and from page 29 of the chapter on "Matter" in Susan Griffin's book, *Woman and Nature: The roaring inside her* (HarperCollins Canada, 1988).

▷ "Hunter/Gatherers" background sources include: *Women's Work: The first 20,000 years*, Elizabeth Wayland Barber (W.W. Norton & Company, 1994); *The Alphabet versus the Goddess*, Leonard Shlain (Penguin Putnam, 1999); *Urgent Message from Mother: Gather the women, save the world*, Jean Bolen (Conari Press, 2005); *Woman and Nature: The roaring inside her*, Susan Griffin (HarperCollins Canada, 1988); *Myth of Matriarchal Prehistory: Why an invented past won't give women a future*, Cynthia Eller (Beacon Press, 2000); *Hemispheric Asymmetry: What's right and what's left*, Joseph Hellige (Harvard University Press, 2001).

▷ In the section under the heading, "Women's Work' around the globe", personal experience provides the foundation. Never having travelled to Saudi Arabia, my understanding of that country's gender experiences has been gleaned from ongoing dialogues with Yemeni sheikhs residing in Saudi, and with Saudi citizens residing outside the Kingdom. King Abdullah's recent modernizations have been well-documented in *The Economist* and in the Western media. An October 26, 2007 *New York Times* article by Thanassis Cambanis, entitled "Saudi King Tries to Grow Modern Ideas in Desert", was particularly helpful. Stephen Lewis's advocacy on gender is well-documented on The Stephen Lewis Foundation website. Norway's experience with gender equality on Boards of Directors is documented in several media communications, including *The Economist* January 5, 2008 edition in an article entitled "Business in Norway: Girl Power". *Time* magazine's December 22, 2002 edition declared Coleen Rowley, Cynthia Cooper and Sherron Watkins, all female whistleblowers, as 2002 Persons of the Year.

▷ Catalyst, a US based think-tank, is an excellent source for research into the question of female participation in the workplace. A 2007 report, *The Double-Bind Dilemma for Women in Leadership: Damned if you do, doomed if you don't,* provides details. Catalyst's website provides very useful research information and background.

▷ Susan Pinker's 2008 book, *Sexual Paradox: Extreme men, gifted women and the real gender gap* (Random House of Canada, 2008), reopens the biology is destiny dialogue on gender and is an excellent resource for the state of the art on scientific research on gender.

▷ In 2001, I conducted interviews with one hundred Western female professionals with at least five years of experience in international business or government sectors, to test perceptions and realities. The feedback was disquieting; the myths about the potential for females in international projects were very different than these females' reality.

▷ Quotes from Sharon McIntryre are used, with permission, based on a July 2008 interview.

▷ Anne Morrow Lindbergh's book, *Gift from the Sea* (Random House, 1955) is a wonderful source of insight on the experiences of females, in particular, the back-and-forth tugs of Victorianism and Feminism.

▷ Legal wrangling on gender discrimination within Morgan Stanley and Merrill Lynch are well-documented in media sources. Legal Momentum is an advocacy non-governmental organization with superb sources available on its website.

▷ The story shared by my friend, Barbara, is published with permission and is based on a true experience.

▷ Under the topic heading, "Underutilized resource?", *The Economist* is an excellent source for detailed information on the economic impacts of gender equality across the globe. The United Nations' reporting is also increasingly explicit; reports can be accessed on the UNIFEM website. Research on gender within individual professions is slowly emerging as a useful source. National industry associations, lawyers' bar associations and accounting institutes have conducted sector-wide research and surveys that can be fairly readily accessed.

▷ Research by Robin Ely and Irene Padavic published in *Academy of Management Review*, 2007, Vol. 32, No. 4, entitled "A Feminist Analysis of Organizational Research on Sex Differences" provides helpful survey information that helps to understand benign assumptions made within organizations.

▷ Research published by University of Cambridge, in 2008, researcher, Professor Jacqueline Scott, finds evidence of "mounting concern" that women who play a full and equal role in the workforce do so at the expense of family life. The study appears in a 2008 book, *Women and Employment: Changing lives and new challenges* edited by Professor Scott. The majority of the contributors form part of an ongoing research network on Gender Inequalities funded by the Economic and Social Research Council (ESRC).

Chapter 4: The Individual within the Community

▷ The three quotes that introduce this chapter are sourced from Joseph Campbell, *The Hero with a Thousand Faces,* Campbell's seminal book of comparative mythology first published in 1949 and the basis of George Lucas's *Star Wars* films; F. David Peat's *Pathways of Chance* (Pari Publishing, 2007); and Mary Wollstonecraft's *A Vindication of the Rights of Woman* written in the late 1700's.

▷ The story of Baby Ali in Seiyun, Yemen, is based on my visit to this hospital with a Bridges' health-care training team in November 2007. I have known, and taught, Dr Ibrahim Al-Kaff over several years and am deeply moved by his dedication to the communities in the Hadhramout.

▷ *New Partnership for Africa's Development* is a strategic vision set by African leaders for their development; the objectives are clearly defined on their host website. The *Arab Human Development Reports* are targets for development established and measured by Arabs within the United Nations Human Development framework; details are available on the UNDP website.

▷ In the section on "Cultural violence against females", several inspirational books on how to effect social change have been used as sources: Chris Turner's book on green environmental practices, *The Geography of Hope: A tour of the world we need* (Random House of Canada, 2007); Malcolm Gladwell's book, *The Tipping Point: How little things can make a big difference* (Back Bay Books, 2002). Other inspirational sources for catalyzing positive change include: *The Starfish and the Spider: The unstoppable power of leaderless organizations* by Ori Brafman and Rod Beckstrom (Penguin, 2006) and *The Power of Unreasonable People: How social entrepreneurs create markets that change the world* by John Elkington and Pamela Hartigan (Harvard Business Press, 2008). These writers inspire me to stay the course, even in the face of the most daunting challenges.

▷ Sigmund Freud's observation on the clitoris is excerpted from his 1931 book, *The Dissection of the Psychical Personality*. The shocking details about the removal of the clitoris of a female toddler by Khalid Adem, an Ethiopian living in the United States, Egyptian experience with female genital mutilation, Indian experience with female infanticide and bride burnings, and Iranian and Saudi treatment of female rape victims are all well documented in the Western media. The Tostan Project has a well-resourced website exploring community-led development.

▷ Reviewing Western experience with cultural violence against women, a quote from Susan Griffin's book, *Women and Nature,* is included to demonstrate the potential for reproductive rights dilemmas. Stephanie Garrett shared her Master's thesis describing her experience in Chile and was a generous resource for dialogue on the question of abortion. Steve Denning is always a trusted resource for insight on storytelling and his book, *The Secret Language of Leadership* (John Wiley & Sons, 2007) provides constructive guidance. The quote from *Maclean's*, by editor Andrew Coyne, was extracted from an article entitled "Dr Morgentaler, the Order of Canada, and the abortion debate we're afraid to have" in the July 21, 2008 edition of the magazine.

▷ The sources for stories of international cultural violence against females are raw; drawn from face-to-face discussions with violated females, and upon the firsthand accounts shared in books by people like Ayaan Hirsi Ali who writes about her youth in Somalia in *Infidel* (Free Press, 2007); Khadija Al-Salami in *Tears of Sheba*; Azar Nafisi in *Reading Lolita in Tehran* (Random House Trade Publishing, 2003); and Khaled Hosseini in *A Thousand Splendid Suns* (Riverhead Books, 2007)—to name but a few.

▷ A quote from *Women Who Run with the Wolves* by Clarissa Pinkola Estes, (Ballantine Books, 1997) is included, as well as Western research on violence against women: *Understanding Violence against Women* published by the American Psychological Association (National Academy Press, 1996) and *Violence Against Women*, edited by Claire Renzetti and Raquel Kennedy Bergen (Rowman & Littlefield, 2005). The provocative question posed in 2006 by Australian-based Muslim cleric, Sheikh Taj el-Din al-Hilali, is well documented in the media and in Bhutto's book, *Reconciliation*.

▷ Sources for views on consumer culture were drawn from a variety of public sources, including Naomi Wolf's book, *The Beauty Myth: How images of beauty are used against women* (Anchor Books, 1991).

▷ Sources for information on maternal and child mortality in Yemen were provided by government and private sources. The United Nations'

Child Rights Convention is available on the UN website. The 2008 report on maternal mortality in Yemen completed by Save the Children Sweden and the Gender Development Research and Studies Center at Sana'a University was kindly made available to Bridges by Dr Jamila al-Raiby, Deputy Minister of Public Health and Population. The Mother's Index 2007 is available on the Save the Children organization's website.

▷ Sufi wisdom on veils is drawn from *The Garden of Truth;* previously referenced. C.S. Lewis' novel, *Till We Have Faces* (William B. Eerdmans Publishing Company, 1956) is an exceptional source of insight on veiling.

▷ *The Economist*, again, provides accurate information on education of males and females, including literacy training impacts. *Three Cups of Tea: One man's mission to promote peace...one school at a time*, by Greg Mortenson and David Oliver Relin (Penguin, 2006), provided insight into the impact of girls' education in Pakistan.

▷ Yemeni colleagues—Dr Adel Bahameed, Dr Abdul-Karim Eryiani, are indefatigable sources of wisdom on Yemeni health care and education priorities for males and females.

Chapter 5: The Individual and Faith

▷ Sources for the quotes preceding this chapter on faith include excerpts from Susan Griffin's book, *Women and Nature* (the first two quotes) and an excerpt from Karen Armstrong's book, *The Gospel According to Women* (Anchor, 1991). Karen Armstrong's writing on inter-faith relationships and understanding are compelling sources; reading her book, *The Battle for God* (Ballantine Books, 2001) has also influenced my interpretation of these issues.

▷ Margaret Atwood is a luminary on these questions; over the decades, many of her books and stories have guided my way of thinking on gender. This chapter on faith includes a very short quote from Atwood's short story, "Third Handed", included in her collection *Good Bones and Simple Murders* (Virago Press, 1993). Atwood's *Handmaid's Tale* (McClelland & Stewart, 1985) is another classic on gender. Atwood's sense of humor is well appreciated. Other Western writers who have applied a sense of humor to these daunting issues, that I would recommend, include: Ann Jones' *Looking for Lovedu: A woman's journey through Africa* (Vintage, 2001) and Alison Wearing's *Honeymoon in Purdah* (Vintage Canada, 2001).

▷ Several faith leaders have mentored me, including Revd Clint Mooney, United Church minister in Canada; Dr Roland Miller, Lutheran missionary in India and author of *Muslim Friends: Their faith and feeling* (Concordia Scholarship Today, 1995); and Cynthia Bourgeault, a former hermetic monk and author of *The Wisdom Way of Knowing: Reclaiming an ancient tradition to awaken the heart* (Jossey-Bass, 2003).

▷ Others whose opinions indirectly influence my observations in this chapter include: Parker Palmer, author of *A Hidden Wholeness* (Jossey-Bass, 2004); Kathleen Norris, author of *The Cloister Walk* (Penguin Books, 1996); Geraldine Brooks, author of *Nine Parts of Desire: The hidden world of Islamic women* (First Anchor Books, 1995).

▷ Gloria Steinem's championing of *Ms.* magazine and Wonder Woman form part of America's well-documented history of feminism. The Rt Revd John Shelby Spong, retired bishop of the Episcopal Diocese of Newark, is a provocative agent for change in the Christian faith community and author of several articles including one entitled "Saint Wonder Woman" from which the quotes referenced in this chapter are excerpted. Spong's articles are available on many websites, including an ecumenical site called beliefnet. Aristotle's quote on gender is widely cast and can be readily extracted from public sources; I referenced several books on Aristotle to confirm consistency. Elizabeth Cady Stanton's stand on religion is public and the quote used in this chapter is very easily accessed on several women's movements websites hosted in the US. The quote of Desmond Tutu's on the Anglican Church in South Africa is extracted from a June 2007 article entitled "God is Weeping" published in an Africa-focused edition of *Vanity Fair*; the article was a conversation between Brad Pitt and Nobel Peace Prize winner Archbishop Desmond Tutu.

▷ Shlain's perspectives on literacy and faith were incorporated into this chapter; Shlain's book, *The Alphabet versus the Goddess*, previously referenced, provided excellent source material. Cynthia Eller's *The Myth of Matriarchal Prehistory*, again provided helpful source material for this chapter.

▷ Meetings with the Sufi faith leader in Yemen and with the ecumenical group of faith leaders in Canada provided rich insight and direct source material for this chapter. Seyyed Hossein Nasr's *The Garden of Truth* helped me to understand Sufi interpretations of the Qur'an, and a quote included in this chapter is from Nasr's book. Osho's quote about the oak tree and the cypress is from *The Book of Wisdom: Discourses on Atisha's seven points of mind training* by Osho (previously referenced).

▷ I picked up the "Welcome to Yemen" tourist brochure in Sana'a Yemen in 2007; the pamphlet was published by the Yemeni Cultural Center for Foreigners.

▷ Unless otherwise noted in the book, excerpts from the Holy Bible are from the King James Version.

▷ The ongoing dialogue between Pope Benedict XVI and a delegation of the 138 Muslim authors of the open letter "A Common Word between Us and You", including their ground rules for dialogue quoted in this chapter, is publicly shared in Western media sources and by the Vatican. Sandro Magister in Rome has been reporting on these exchanges, openly and credibly; a quick internet search of his name will unearth many of his articles recording the ongoing inter-faith dialogue.

▷ Other sources for this chapter include excerpts from Oliver Roy's book, *Secularism Confronts Islam,* translated by George Holoch (Columbia University Press, 2007); and from Ayaan Hirsi Ali's *Infidel* (previously referenced). Tariq Ramadan's views on Islam are widely accessible in the Western media. Khaled Hosseini's *A Thousand Splendid Suns* (previously referenced) is quoted directly.

▷ Cultural Issues with Concerned Women for America and the Tandem Project host websites that are readily accessible. Riffat Hassan's excellent article, "Members, One of Another: Gender equality and justice in Islam" (Department of Religious Studies, University of Louisville) was the source of thinking on Islamic interpretations of gender equality; a quote from her article is included in the chapter.

▷ Thomas Homer-Dixon's book, *The Upside of Down* (Knopf Canada, 2006) is referenced. The 2007 statement on Al Jazeera television by Wafa Sultan, an Arab-American psychologist from Los Angeles, criticizing Islam's backwardness in its treatment of women was removed from their website. Sam Harris' *The End of Faith* (Free Press, 2005) is also used as a source.

▷ My personal experience with Nadia, the fundamentalist teacher from Ta'iz Yemen, happened in May 2005; all aspects of this story are true.

Chapter 6: The Individual within the Family

▷ The wedding story is based on personal experience; names of Yemeni females participating in the wedding party have been intentionally excluded to respect cultural norms about modesty.

▷ Quotes by Virginia Woolf and Margaret Atwood—visionaries—precede this chapter on gender and family. The Virginia Woolf quote on the greatness of the androgynous mind is from her seminal book, *A Room of One's Own*, originally published in 1929 by Hogarth Press.

The Margaret Atwood quote is from her short story, "Alien Territory" published in *Good Bones and Simple Murders* (previously referenced).

▷ Leonard Shlain's book, *Alphabet versus the Goddess* (previously referenced) is again a source, as well as Joseph Campbell's wisdom on marriage and consciousness.

▷ Dr Laura Schlessinger's book, *The Proper Care and Feeding of Husbands* (HarperCollins, 2004) is referenced, and Schlessinger's quote about Mrs. Spitzer was sourced from Schlessinger's comments on the *Today* show in March 2008. The quote by Ellen Goodman, columnist in the *Boston Globe*, was extracted from her March 14, 2008 article on Spitzer, "Political wives forced to pay a dear price".

▷ The observations on differences between belonging and enterprise values were derived from Carol Lee Flinders' work in *Rebalancing the World: Why women belong and men compete and how to restore the ancient equilibrium* (Harper, 2002).

▷ The short excerpt from Margaret Atwood's "The Little Red Hen Tells All" story is from her story collection, *Good Bones and Simple Murders* (previously referenced).

▷ The experiences in Yemen are based on fifteen years of personal engagement with Yemeni families, within their homes and personal lives.

▷ The experiences in China are based on a family visit to China in the summer of 2007. Quotes from local Chinese newspapers are taken directly, as are quotes from individual Chinese men and women.

▷ The final quote, by Martin Buber, is excerpted from his book, *I and Thou: Martin Buber*, a new translation with a Prologue and Notes by Walter Kaufman, (Simon & Schuster, 1970).

Chapter 7: Creating a breathing space

▷ The first quote is from the New American Standard Bible; this translation is preferred given the language of crocuses blooming. This is the Bible verse that brought the image of *flowers blooming in the desert* to life for me. The second quote, by William Irwin Thompson, is borrowed by Leonard Shlain's *The Alphabet versus the Goddess*. The third quote, on the space between stimulus and response, is from Viktor E. Frankl, a Nazi death camp survivor, psychologist, and author of *Man's Search for Meaning* (Pocket, 1997).

▷ Eckhart Tolle's book, *A New Earth: Awakening to your life's purpose* (Plume, 2005) provided great inspiration for several quotes in this chapter.

▷ The quote on breathing, by an ancient Indian Tantra, was referred to by Helen Luke in *Kaleidoscope* (previously referenced) and is frequently quoted in Eastern literature. Carl Sagan's *Cosmos* was a source (Ballantine Books, 1985). *Shah of Shahs* by Ryszard Kapuscinski (Vintage International, 1992), an English translation, is also referenced. References to liminal space were drawn from Lord Dunsany's 1924 book, *The King of Elfland's Daughter* (Del Rey, 1999).

▷ The issue of complexity is supported with reference to *Getting to Maybe*, by authors Frances Westley, Brenda Zimmerman and Michael Patton (Random House, 2006), and to Bill Gates' 2007 address to the graduating class at Harvard. Gates' speech is accessible on YouTube and on the Bill & Melinda Gates Foundation website.

▷ Rebecca Solnit's imagery—wielding hope like an axe—in her book, *Hope in the Dark* (Penguin, 2006) was rousing. The interview with Flora Macdonald was equally inspirational; these quotes by Ms. Macdonald are used with permission.

▷ Several references are made to Eastern and Jungian beliefs and principles: The Confucian belief that a teacher is one *who can reanimate the old to know the new;* Lao-tzu use of the metaphor of horizontally flowing water; and Jungian links between spirit and water.

▷ The Pueblo Indian images referred to in this chapter were sourced from *Ambiguous Images: Gender and rock art*, by Kelley A. Hays-Gilpin (AltaMira Press, 2004).

▷ Conversations with Dr Bernie Novokowsky were the catalyst for much deeper thinking on two-ness, one-ness and the value of a third element.

▷ Martin Buber's *I and Thou* wisdom was sourced from his book, *I and Thou* (previously referenced).

▷ The concept of "Dialogue among Civilizations" is a theory of international relations advocated by the former President of Iran, Mohammed Khatami, as a response to Samuel Huntington's theory of the "Clash of Civilizations". Quotes in this chapter by Khatami are sourced from his 2000 address to the United Nations; this speech influenced the United Nations to name the year 2001 as the year of Dialogue among Civilizations. The Geneva-based Foundation for Dialogue Among Civilizations is an international foundation established in 2007 to promote the institution of regular dialogue between the world's peoples, cultures, civilizations and religions in order to promote peace, justice and tolerance.

▷ Farid Esack is a South African Muslim academic, author and activist; the referenced quote by Esack on victimhood is from a November 2004 feature interview with John Cleary on an ABC *Sunday Night*. Esack's writings can be readily accessed online.

▷ The final quote of this chapter is Carlo Levi's famous line: *the future has an ancient heart*. This was the title of a 1956 book published by Levi in Italy *(Il Futuro ha un Cuore Antico; The Future has an Ancient Heart)*. It was affirming to me that this Levi quote had also become the maxim of the Pari Center founded by F. David Peat in Italy.

Chapter 8: Raising Sons

▷ The introductory quotes to this chapter include a short excerpt from Marie-Louise von Franz's *Animus and Anima in Fairy Tales;* and Susan Griffin's *Woman and Nature: The roaring inside her.*

▷ Much of this chapter is derived from personal experience and observations, enriched through dialogue with experts like Dr Jagdeep Johal, other mothers of sons and daughters, and even my own mother.

▷ Shlain's *The Alphabet versus the Goddess* was again a useful source. Michael Gurian's book, *Mothers, Sons, and Lovers* (Shambhala, 1993) is cited, as well as research by anthropologist, Sherry Ortner. Several academic websites showcase Ortner's research including her article entitled, "Is Female to Male as Nature Is to Culture?" (Stanford University Press, 1974), from which the quote included in this chapter was extracted.

▷ The song "White Sahara" is on Canadian singer Susan Aglukark's *Big Feeling* album.

▷ Although not directly sourced, other books that provided some insight into the questions explored in this chapter include: William Pollack's book, *Real Boys: Rescuing our sons from the myths of boyhood* (Random House, 1998); John Gray's classic, *Men Are from Mars, Women Are from Venus: A practical guide for improving communication and getting what you want in your relationships* (HarperCollins, 1992); and *Raising Cain: Protecting the emotional life of boys* by Dan Kindlon and Michael Thompson (Ballantine, 2000).

▷ The final quote is an excerpt from John Donne's poem, "The Good-Morrow", extracted from *Poems of John Donne*, Volume 1, edited by E.K. Chambers (Lawrence & Bullen, 1896).

Epilogue

▷ The Rumi quote is from a poem entitled "Longing for the Birds of Solomon" translated by Robert Bly and included in *The Rumi Collection*

edited by Kabir Helminski (Shambhala Classics, 2000). The next line
of this couplet is: *Those who hear the note feel an intensity in their whole
body.*

▷ The story of Ahlam is accurate; including the wording of the email
note sent to me.

Color Illustrations

The Bird Necklace

▷ The photo of the Bird Necklace was taken by a Yemeni friend,
and jewelry designer, Walid Rubaih of Sana'a, Yemen. The necklace was
crafted by a Yemenite Jew, Yihye al-Abyadh, between 1930 and 1940
for the Muslim population in Sana'a. In her book, *The Yemenites: Two
thousand years of Jewish culture* (Israel Museum, 2000), Ester Muchawsky-
Schnapper explains the role of Yemenite Jews in Yemen and the concept
of *baraka*, the belief that jewelry made by a foreigner possesses a special
blessing. This book, full of photos and stories, sits on my coffee table and
offers endless satisfaction.

Your Role in Advancing Gender Harmonization

Your purchase of this book directly supports gender harmonization. All royalties from the sale of this book will be dedicated to advancing gender harmonization through the volunteer work of Bridges Social Development (www.canadabridges.com).

As well, workbooks have been created as guides to help you understand, and talk about, the gender dilemmas explored in this book. These workbooks will help you peel your own Gender Onion, as an individual reader or together with others. If you belong to a book club, professional organization, company, community group, not-for-profit organization, individual church congregation or faith group, inter-faith dialogue group or student group, you may want to download one or all of these workbooks to guide your exploration of a particular layer of the Gender Onion. You may even use these workbooks to discuss gender equality dilemmas within your own family.

There are seven workbooks: An Introductory Workbook to explain the Gender Onion idea; five workbooks to guide you through the five layers of the Gender Onion; and a final workbook to help you write your own story about gender equality and breathing spaces.

These workbooks are available to you at no cost. You can download them from these websites: www.canadabridges.com; www.unveilingthebreath.com; www.paripublishing.com and www.paricenter.com. If you find these workbooks helpful, please consider making a charitable donation to Bridges Social Development. Your donation will be used to advance this volunteer organization's role in supporting gender harmonization on a global basis. Links are available on these websites to explain how online donations can be made.

Introductory Workbook	Seeing the layers of your Gender Onion	Introducing the layers of the Gender Onion
Red Workbook	Seeing yourself in the World	Understanding your worldview... your place in the world
Orange Workbook	Seeing yourself at Work	Navigating gender dilemmas in the workplace
Green Workbook	Seeing yourself within your Community	Expectations about health and education; cultural violence
Blue Workbook	Seeing yourself in your Faith	Reconciling faith and spirituality expectations
Purple Workbook	Seeing yourself in your Family	Family expectations and relationships
Gold Workbook	Finding your "little kernel of gold"	Your story: Creating your own breathing spaces

Pari Publishing is an independent publishing company, based in a medieval Italian village. Our books appeal to a broad readership and focus on innovative ideas and approaches from new and established authors who are experts in their fields. We publish books in the areas of science, society, psychology, and the arts.

Our books are available at all good bookstores or online at
www.paripublishing.com

If you would like to add your name to our email list to receive information about our forthcoming titles and our online newsletter please contact us at **newsletter@paripublishing.com**

Visit us at **www.paripublishing.com**

Pari Publishing Sas
Via Tozzi, 7
58045 Pari (GR)
Italy

Email: info@paripublishing.com